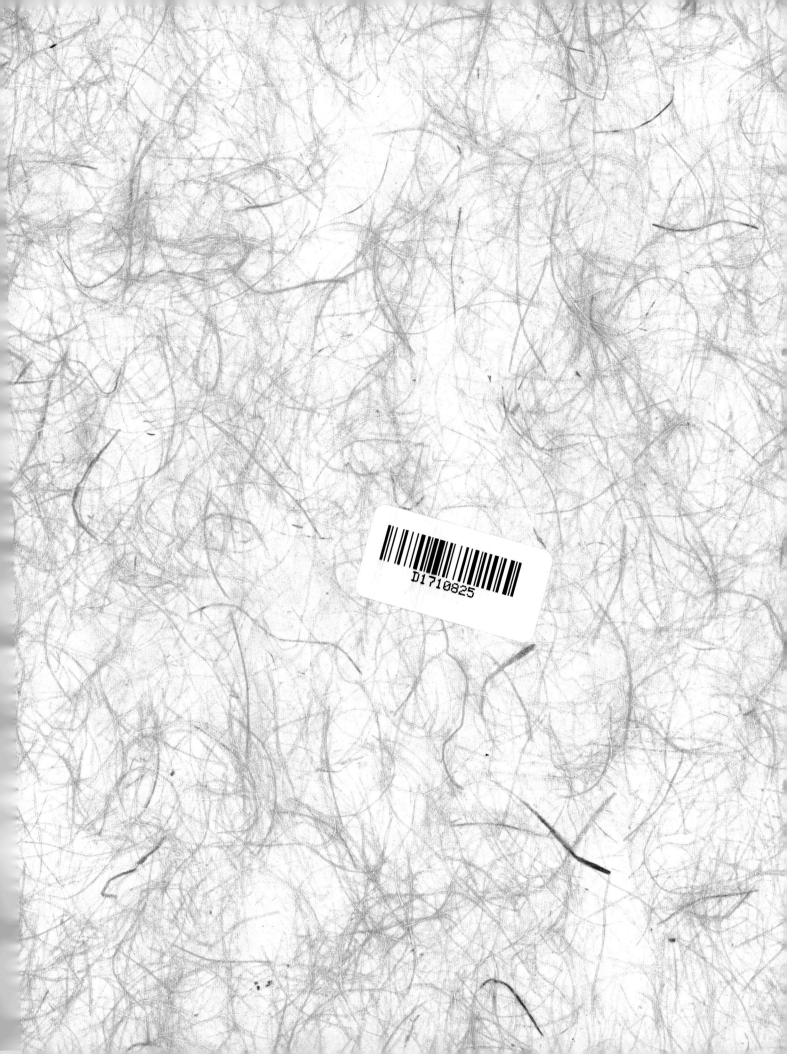

Wedgwood Ceramics

Daniel J. Keefe III

Front cover photographed by Albie Walton

4880 Lower Valley Road, Atglen, PA 19310 USA

Dedication

To my wife, Vanessa: for all her hard work in helping me
put this book together and the patience, support, and
understanding to help me see it through.

Library of Congress Cataloging-in-Publication Data

Keefe, Daniel J., III.
  Wedgwood ceramics / Daniel J. Keefe III ; front and back
cover photographed by Albie Walton.
    p. cm.
  ISBN 0-7643-2298-2 (hardcover)
  1. Wedgwood ware. I. Title.

NK4335K37 2006
738.3'09424'63--dc22

                    2005020546

Designed by Mark David Bowyer
Type set in University Roman Bd BT/Souvenir Lt BT

ISBN: 0-7643-2298-2
Printed in China
1 2 3 4

Published by Schiffer Publishing Ltd.
4880 Lower Valley Road
Atglen, PA 19310
Phone: (610) 593-1777; Fax: (610) 593-2002
E-mail: Info@schifferbooks.com

For the largest selection of fine reference books on this and
related subjects, please visit our web site at
www.schifferbooks.com
We are always looking for people to write books on new
and related subjects. If you have an idea for a book please
contact us at the above address.

This book may be purchased from the publisher.
Include $3.95 for shipping.
Please try your bookstore first.
You may write for a free catalog.

In Europe, Schiffer books are distributed by
Bushwood Books
6 Marksbury Ave.
Kew Gardens
Surrey TW9 4JF England
Phone: 44 (0) 20 8392-8585; Fax: 44 (0) 20 8392-9876
E-mail: info@bushwoodbooks.co.uk
Free postage in the U.K., Europe; air mail at cost.

Contents

Acknowledgments

A grateful thank you to the following contributors for allowing me to come into their homes and photograph their beautiful collections that are so close to their hearts: Robert Chellis and Sandy Adams, Ronald F. Frazier, Kenneth Goldman, Jeffrey Hoffman and Lorraine Horn, Donald Eric Johnson, Dorothy-Lee Jones, Daniel and Mary Keefe, Whitney Milan, Beverly Rosen, Stuart Slavid.

In addition, a special note of thanks to Jeffrey Hoffman, Lorraine Horn, Dorothy-Lee Jones, Stuart Slavid, and Lynn Miller for providing guidance on this project, especially Ronald F. Frazier, my Wedgwood mentor.

A special thank you to Albie Walton and Forrest Frazier for photography and technical guidance, and Dan and Mary Keefe for their support of my collection.

Preface

If it could be made in a ceramic body, it is probable that Josiah Wedgwood and those who followed in his company would make it. Both useful and decorative wares: from the mortar and pestle, to the chamber pot and bidet, tobacco pipes, to the finest Bone China, to magnificent vases and statuaries in Basalt and Jasper. Of course, the most widely known and recognizable product invented by Josiah Wedgwood was Jasper Ware, familiar to even the uninitiated for its familiar light blue background and white relief.

Wedgwood's manufacturing history spans more than 245 years and during that time virtually millions of different products, bodies, shapes, and designs have been made. Most authors focus on one specific area about which to write. For this reason, Daniel Keefe's book was a monumental task, as it covers products from the time the Wedgwood company was founded to the present day. Dan chose to feature collections in the New England area, owned mainly by members of the Wedgwood Society of Boston. That being said, these New England collections, in private hands, contain some of the most important and magnificent products made by Wedgwood.

Dan's awareness of Wedgwood began as a teenager when he came to live with my family for several years as a friend of my son. Virtually every room in our home contained some form of Wedgwood. Several years after he moved from our home, Dan called me and asked if he could visit. At that point, he had been haunting an-

tique shops and had decided what interested him and that what he wanted to collect was Wedgwood.

Dan began his own collection and extensive library, and became an officer in the Wedgwood Society of Boston. He then joined the Wedgwood International Seminar, as well as a number of other related organizations. As a young man, he has had the great fortune of knowing world-renowned collectors and their collections, including Elizabeth Chellis (collection now held by Robert Chellis and Sandy Adams), Lloyd and Vivian Hawes, Jeffrey Hoffman and Lorraine Horn, Beverly and Benton Rosen, and Dorothy-Lee Jones, among others. As part of the Wedgwood Society of Boston, all of these people were, and are, eager to share their knowledge and help those who have an interest in Wedgwood ceramics.

Having worked on several books myself, I know the time and dedication that is involved in such a project. While Dan has a wealth of experience as a collector of Wedgwood, having been collecting nearly half his life, he took on this new venture with a vitality that few who also have a regular business career would even consider. (Ah, the exuberance of youth!) While some of the privately-owned items shown in this book have appeared in scholarly publications due to their importance, the vast majority have not until now, therefore making this book a valuable asset to anyone interested in the broad range of Wedgwood ceramics and decorative arts.

— Ronald Forrest Frazier

Introduction

Too often people view Wedgwood as the company that makes "all those blue and white collectibles." Though the "blue and whites" are extremely popular, easy to recognize, and plentiful in supply, they simply do not do justice to the true depth and breadth of Wedgwood's creations.

What then is Wedgwood? Wedgwood is a versatile collection of ceramics that covers virtually every aspect you can imagine. They range from the traditional blue and white decorative pieces, to tablewares, Victorian Art Pottery, busts and statuaries, massive hand-painted decorative vases, and tiny ornate trinket boxes. Wedgwood is also Commemorative Ware, animal sculptures, Chamber Ware, medical instruments, Portrait Medallions, kitchen tiles, and futuristic, Art Deco-styled sculptures and ceramics. Put simply, Wedgwood's 'blue and white' is just the tip of the iceberg.

My passion for collecting focuses on exploring this wide range of Wedgwood, especially the unusual and eclectic pieces that most would never even think of as being Wedgwood. I also believe that an essential aspect to collecting Wedgwood is understanding the "big picture." This "big picture" can be in a physical sense of course, such as the how the pottery was formed and what clays make up the mixtures. Sometimes, a more interesting facet to Wedgwood is exploring the cultural and historical influences on the company's products.

My overall purpose of this book is to share my enthusiasm for the wide range of Wedgwood wares that exist. I would like to help you identify these more unusual pieces and understand how they came to be part of Wedgwood. I have included a sampling of the full spectrum of products that Wedgwood has produced during the past two hundred years, from one-of-a-kind works of art to some of the more modern items with which new collectors typically start their collections. I would also like to help you explore the history and stories that surround Wedgwood's wares since many of these stories are just as rare and usual as the pieces themselves.

— Daniel J. Keefe III

Print of The Wedgwood and Byerley Showroom at York Street, St. James' Square, London, England. From Ackerman's Repository of Arts. Published 1809.

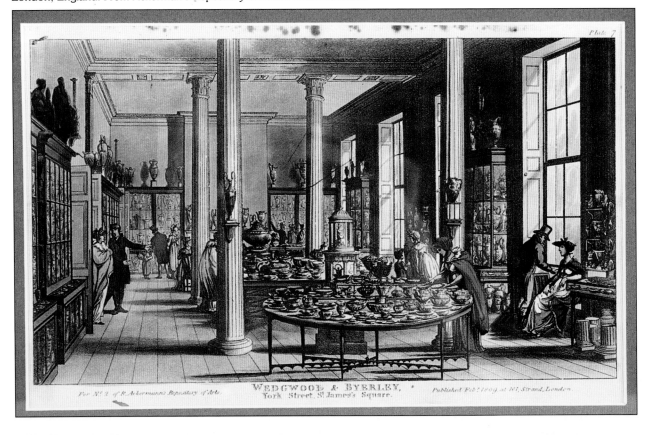

Chapter 1
Earthenware

In the mid-1700s, Josiah Wedgwood performed his first experiments with earthenware. The term Earthenware refers to pottery made from a simple clay and water mixture. When fired, the clay develops a hardened, porous surface that requires glazing to make it impenetrable to liquids. At the time Wedgwood was founding his company, earthenware served as a rudimentary pottery form widely used for making tableware. It was with earthenware that Josiah Wedgwood would make his first groundbreaking innovation.

Green Glazed Ware

In the 1760s, Josiah Wedgwood first gained public recognition through his early innovations with Green Glazed Ware, a cream-colored earthenware ceramic that has been partially fired, coated with a green lead-based glaze, and then re-fired to achieve a translucent, glossy finish. Though this process was used in Staffordshire, England, for a number of years prior to Wedgwood's time, Wedgwood experimented with refining and improving the color qualities of the glaze as well as trying new ceramic shapes. Wedgwood approached pottery not only from a utilitarian standpoint, but also as an art form.

Thomas Whieldon, an important and influential potter of the time, had long been producing cream-colored wares with glazes of black, grey, brown, blue and green. In 1754, Wedgwood entered into a five-year partnership with Whieldon in an effort to improve his knowledge and understanding of ceramics. Building on Whieldon's knowledge, Wedgwood was able to take glazed earthenware in new and creative directions.

Glazed Earthenware: Tortoiseshell Ware

Tortoiseshell Ware was a Whieldon innovation produced by combining his green and brown glazes in a random speckled, tortoiseshell-like pattern on earthenware tea sets. This blending of colors was new and different, and quickly caught the public's eye. Its success inspired Wedgwood to experiment with glazes in ways that Whieldon was less inclined to explore. Wedgwood made a similar mottled-looking ware using a different blending process. He would sprinkle coloring oxides on the ceramic before firing, which would then melt under the heat of the kiln and run together in streak-like patterns. With the combination of green and yellow glazes, Wedgwood also produced a tortoiseshell effect similar to Whieldon's earlier design. He produced these glazed wares at the same time as Whieldon, often utilizing similar styles and themes.

Teapot in cauliflower shape, c. 1763. Green Glazed Ware with yellow glazing on top. This piece is not marked, but has been authenticated. *Courtesy of the Chellis and Adams Collection.* $1,000-1,100.

Glazed Earthenware: Fruits & Vegetables

Wedgwood's introduction of yellow glaze in 1760 led to new multi-colored possibilities; in particular, Josiah was very successful with his pineapple and cauliflower wares. The ceramic shapes, mainly comprised of tea ware sets, were formed to resemble the texture and contours of the fruits and vegetables for which they were named. The colored glazes Wedgwood used helped to make them truly realistic and bring them to life.

The cauliflower and pineapple tea shapes were some of the first wares that Wedgwood's company produced as an independent entity, and the cauliflower and pineapple were the most popular of the fruit and vegetable shapes. Other shapes included pears, apples, melons, artichokes, and cabbage forms. These designs were more realistic and colorful than Whieldon's glazed creations. The fruits and vegetable style was fresh, creative, and well received by the public, as well as by other potters who quickly mimicked Wedgwood's designs.

Wedgwood halted production of wares coated with Green Glaze in 1776; competing potters, who had blatantly copied his work, had saturated the market. As occurred in many stages of Wedgwood's history, once a Wedgwood style grabbed the public's attention and sold well, other potters were quick to capitalize on Wedgwood's success by flooding the market with inexpensive, lesser quality copies.

Wedgwood briefly began production again on the Green Glazed Ware in 1779 for decoration of flowerpots. The yellow glaze, which he used primarily with the green glaze, continued off and on in limited quantities until c. 1833. Green Glazed Ware also saw a revival later in the late 1800s for leaf-shaped desert services and shell-motifs during Wedgwood's Majolica production, and again in a revival of the cauliflower and pineapple wares in 1920-1930. These more recent fruit and vegetable designs differed from the originals as they were mass-produced and lacked the fine quality of their earlier hand-made counterparts.

Salt-Glazed Stoneware

Salt-glazing was an early method of protective glazing that had been used in Germany since the fourteenth century and migrated to the English potteries in the 1730s. After heating a clay piece to a desired temperature, potters threw common salt into the fire, where it volatilized and combined with the silica and aluminum oxides in the clay. This resulted in a thin deposit of glass, or glaze coating, on the surface of the piece. This often gave the surface of the finished product a slightly pitted texture.

Wedgwood utilized salt-glazing in his company's early years, but most of these early salt-glazed pieces were unmarked as Wedgwood wares. This of course makes authentication difficult, however the key to identifying these unmarked pieces is knowing the shapes and designs produced for salt-glazed pieces. The close working relationship between Josiah Wedgwood and Thomas Whieldon further complicates the identification process, as wares and styles sometimes criss-crossed between the two potters' companies. This section includes a few unmarked salt-glazed items, authenticated as Wedgwood though they could easily be attributed to either Wedgwood or Whieldon, since the designs were known to have been produced by both potters. A good approach in purchasing unmarked pieces is to know the source. If the seller is a trusted source, they should offer a guarantee that says they will take the piece back if it fails authentication.

Salt-glazing did not last at Wedgwood due in part to the hazardous nature of the production process. The salt-glazing process produced messy and hazardous dense clouds of smoke and chlorine gas from the kilns, which were noxious and harmful to the potters. In addition, the process made the wares susceptible to crackling (surface stress cracks in the glaze) due to variations in cooling temperatures be-

Fruit Plate, c. 1759-1765. Salt-glazed stoneware (pre-Creamware) with raised basket pattern. This plate is not marked, but has been authenticated. It is believed to have been part of Josiah Wedgwood's early salt-glaze experiments. *Courtesy of the Frazier Collection.* $500-700.

tween the glaze and the clay underbody. The advent of Wedgwood's new Creamware in 1760 rendered salt-glazing obsolete and Wedgwood's production of salt-glazed wares ended c. 1763.

Variegated Ware

Variegated Ware is an earthenware pottery that simulates the look of classical antique vases made from polished precious or semi-precious hard-stones like marble or agate. Wedgwood used this form primarily for producing vases, but also made bough (flower) pots, urns, and other decorative pieces using techniques learned during his time with Thomas Whieldon. Variegated Wares were another of Josiah Wedgwood's first products when he opened his new pottery factory in 1759 and one that remained in limited production off and on into the 1900s.

Variegated Ware was an inexpensive substitute for the long and laborious process of digging semi-precious stones out of the earth, then chiseling and polishing the hard stone into works of art. Wedgwood created the same look and feel of these antique stone vases on a cream-colored earthenware body using two decorative techniques: solid agate and surface glazing. Each process simulated the style, look, and patterns of naturally occurring polished stone.

Solid Agate, the first of Wedgwood's Variegated Wares, was more time consuming as it required extra labor by skilled potters to work the clay on a potter's wheel. The key to solid agate was in wedging the different tinted clays together, while being careful to maintain the veining. Colors included brown, yellow, gray, and white. This was an expensive method due to the labor involved, but it resulted in some breathtaking, one-of-a-kind creations. Wedgwood also produced a marbled style in the same manner, but it was less pronounced that the agate. Marbled wares remained in production for only a short time, ceasing in 1800. The technique used for solid agate was revived in limited production during the beginning of the twenty-first century on a variety of Jasper Ware pieces.

In 1759, Wedgwood employed a surface glaze technique at the same time as the solid agate that created a similar effect without requiring the additional labor of skilled potters. Tinted clay slip was blended on a plain creamware body to achieve the same result. This was a faster and easier method than throwing clay by hand and allowed for additional design options. The various surface glazes produced included surface agate glaze, tortoiseshell, porphyry, granite, and pebble — all imitative of natural hard stones that were popular at the time for their decorative colorings and veining. To distinguish between pieces utilizing the solid or surface methods, just look inside the piece. The surface glazed wares have a plain creamware underbody and will have an uncoated interior, whereas the solid wares will have the colored veining throughout the piece. Production of this surface glaze continued until 1900.

The tortoiseshell effect was a Variegated Ware style similar to that of the mottled look. It had its roots back to Thomas Whieldon's Tortoiseshell Ware that he made using his colored glazes. Tortoiseshell was introduced in about 1754, utilizing colored-slips painted-on or sponged-on to the cream-colored surface. Then during firing, the colors would run or flood into the clear glaze creating the tortoiseshell effect.

Creating the porphyry effect involved sprinkling purplish, reddish brown or mottled green-colored slips on a piece, a few rare pieces also utilized white or red. A cloth was sometimes used in place of sprinkling to dab colors on the surface. Other times, metallic coloring oxides were dusted onto the vase before firing to achieve the porphyry effect. Granite styled Variegated Ware was a similar form, but with a mottled grayish-blue coloring. Pebble was a Variegated Ware surface glaze, applied by spraying the ceramic body with metallic oxides prior to glazing.

Covered Vase with handles, c. 1769-1780. Variegated Solid Agate, Mark: "WEDGWOOD & BENTLEY." *Courtesy of the Chellis and Adams Collection.* $3,000-3,500.

Hunt jug, c. 1940. Green Glazed Ware, a twentieth century example, hound-shaped handle, 4.5". *Author's Collection.* $100-125.

Two early salt-glaze fruit plates, c. 1759-1765. These are both unmarked, but they have been authenticated, 8.25" and 10". *Courtesy of the Chellis and Adams Collection.* $500-800 each.

Two salt glaze teapots, (left) c. 1760-1763 and (right) c. 1760-1763. Both are in the Landskip pattern, one with enamel painted colors. Both of these are unmarked, but have been authenticated. *Courtesy of the Chellis and Adams Collection. (Left)* $800-1,000; (right) $750-950.

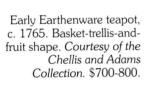

Early Earthenware teapot, c. 1765. Basket-trellis-and-fruit shape. *Courtesy of the Chellis and Adams Collection.* $700-800.

Early cream-colored Earthenware teapot, c. mid-1700s. Hunting scene in black. *Courtesy of the Chellis and Adams Collection.* $700-800.

11

Earthenware teapot, c. 1775. Decorated with flowers, painted by John Rhodes. *Courtesy of the Chellis and Adams Collection.* $1,500-2,000.

Granite Ware, c. 1768-1780. Variegated covered vase (Wedgwood & Bentley mark). *Courtesy of the Goldman Collection.* $3,800-4,100.

Chapter 2
Creamware / Queen's Ware

One of Josiah Wedgwood's largest contributions to the history of ceramics came through his refinement of cream-colored earthenware, which he referred to as Creamware. Creamware had existed before Wedgwood's time, but found use primarily in everyday tableware and was light brown in color, rather than cream, as the name would suggest. Most English potters produced some form of Creamware, none of which were of any great quality and certainly not capable of decorative applications. Wedgwood saw these early wares as unsuitable for his needs, as they chipped easily and the glaze often flaked off. These wares were the best available to the public at the time, unless one was able to pay extremely high prices to have superior quality tableware imported from China. It was for this reason that Wedgwood turned his focus to working out a solution to answer the public's growing demand for whiter, more durable, and overall better quality Creamware.

Wedgwood focused solely on his Creamware experiments, putting in many hours working with local-area Staffordshire clays. Though he had many failed attempts and setbacks, he persisted. In his attempts to improve Creamware, Wedgwood worked to improve every detail of the process, from the potting tools of the day, to the glazes, and he even ended up improving upon the quality of the kilns used. Through these efforts, Wedgwood finally produced a new Creamware body that was of better quality and durable for use as tableware and in the kitchen.

Plat de ménage or épergnes with braided-handled cups, c. 1780. Large table centerpiece with hanging sweet meat baskets, topped with an ornamental pineapple shape. *Courtesy of the Chellis and Adams Collection.* $1,200-1,400.

Now that Wedgwood's Creamware was durable enough, the next aspect he needed to keep consistent was the coloring. His Creamware unfortunately varied from a deep straw color to near white. In some cases, the wares even came out yellow with a slight green or blue tint depending on the cobalt oxide content, which was an ingredient added to the clay formula to whiten the finished product. (Wedgwood eventually encouraged these discolorations and combined them with new designs, naming the tinted pottery Pearl Ware to separate them from his Creamware patterns.) Consumer demand dictated whiter and whiter wares, which were often problematic for Wedgwood to achieve. Curious hues and shades would come out of a single factory, which makes it impossible for collectors to evaluate pieces factory origins by color alone. After additional experimentation, Wedgwood refined his processes and mixtures achieving the consistent evenness in color the market demanded. For the first time, customers knew they could order a piece or setting from different factory batches and the pieces would match when they appeared together on the table.

Another Wedgwood distinction of the time was Creamware's lightness in weight. The lightness was driven by esthetics (lighter being more fashionable and considered a higher quality by the consumer) and out of a need to reduce transportation costs, which were driven by the weight of the product. Wedgwood's Creamware also established a level of quality not previously achieved on tableware. Plates for example, nested perfectly together, lids and tops fit properly, and handles held with strength that matched their purpose. Wedgwood's Creamware items were not only built better, but they were artistic in design — a trait that many of Wedgwood's competitors had not even contemplated.

Queen's Ware

In the mid-1700s while Wedgwood was introducing his new Creamware, England's aristocracy, in which the Royal Family played a pivotal role, set the precedents for style and fashion. Wedgwood never wanted his wares labeled as elitist or only for royalty, but it was from the

Early teapot, c. 1761-1762. Cream-colored earthenware teapot with scrolled handle (predates Wedgwood's refined Creamware) with transfer printed porcelain of Queen Charlotte of England on one side and King George on the other. This piece is not marked, but has been authenticated as being one of Josiah Wedgwood's earliest Creamware pieces. The design was copied from an engraving by F. G. Aliamet. *Courtesy of the Chellis and Adams Collection.* $2,400-2,500.

aristocracy that the Wedgwood name received its largest push into the consciousness of the public.

Wedgwood's new cream-colored body ornamented with green and gold, imitating Dresden-style china, caught the attention of England's Queen Charlotte. This led to an order by the Queen in a shape and style that later became know as the Queen's Pattern or Royal Pattern. The King and Queen were so taken with the Wedgwood set that she named Wedgwood, "Her Majesty's Potter." In 1766, Queen Charlotte, wife of George III, christened Wedgwood's Creamware "Queen's Ware." This honor became a tremendous marketing tool for Wedgwood that grew the company's reputation internationally, in addition to that of Josiah Wedgwood, now officially known as a master potter. The Queen's Ware name would continue to bring Wedgwood great fame and boost his company to enormous heights of success. Unfortunately, only a few rare pieces are known to have survived from this historical first Queen's Ware tea set or of the subsequent dinner service.

By 1766, Wedgwood had his Queen's Ware, as it was now known, in full production, selling a wide range of shapes from small tea sets to large table services. His wares had become so popular that all cream-colored wares produced used the name 'Creamware' even though over 100 potters made similar cream-colored designs. Wedgwood's Queen's Ware also became the driving force behind the demand for English cream-colored ware around the world.

Transfer Printing

Wedgwood introduced transfer printing on Queen's Ware in 1761. This was a technique first invented by John Sadler in 1752 and officially patented in 1754. It involved engraving a design into a reverse-mold, then coating the mold with a mixture of heated color oxide and oil. The image was then impressed onto paper and then "transferred" on top of a pre-glazed plate or other pottery shape, then the piece was re-fired at a lower temperature in an enameling kiln. Typical ink colors used during this period were black, burnt red, brown, purple, and green. This process allowed Wedgwood to begin mass-production of the same design, a faster process than the traditional hand-painted method. However, both methods remained in use into the mid-1900s.

Though the transferring process gradually improved over the years, problems remained. The process still required highly skilled artists to engrave the reverse molds and this process took a significant investment of time. Another issue was that the piece had to be fired in an enameling kiln to solidify the printed image. Josiah Wedgwood II eventually utilized underglaze techniques to improve the process (Josiah Wedgwood passed away in 1795, leaving his son Josiah Wedgwood II to continue with his legacy and passion for pottery).

Plate in the Royal shape, c. 1770-1775. Transfer printed Aesop Fables design, adapted from a series of tiles, border of flower sprays, 9.75". *Courtesy of the Slavid Collection.* $700-900.

Underglazing

The process of applying a design under a glaze prior to firing was already in use in the early 1800s by other potters as well in other countries, particularly China. Josiah Wedgwood II however did not immediately seize on this approach because early experiments tended to turn the clay green and often distorted the image on the Queen's Ware. Wedgwood did have some success applying the method to Pearl Ware, a derivative of Creamware, which worked better as a medium for underglaze. Additionally, Wedgwood felt that he needed to distinguish his wares from the popular tin-glazed items produced by his competitors. The tin-glaze was an opaque glaze utilizing tin oxide to color the glaze white.

Things changed however when Chinese wares started growing in popularity, utilizing a blue underglaze. The Chinese wares were commonly decorated with oriental scenery and reflections of their culture. Recognizing the financial risk of ignoring this growing trend, Wedgwood modified the Queen's Ware formula to make it suitable for similar designs and Oriental style adornments. In 1805, Wedgwood introduced a Queen's Ware variation whose composition closely resembled that of Pearl Ware. Like the Pearl Ware, this modified Queen's Ware incorporated more white clay and flint in the formula (flint being a silica-based form of quartz with water molecules that aided in strength and color), and was fired at higher temperatures to prevent the image from blurring.

One of Wedgwood first attempts with the blue underglaze was his Water Lilly pattern in 1806, first on Pearl Ware to avoid discoloration of the blue print and later on Queen's Ware. The Water Lilly pattern began on Queen's Ware in shades of rust, brown, and gold, which caused less color distortion problems. They were later replaced with blue in 1811 when the process was further refined. The early 1800s saw a red and a multicolored version, but very little information exists on these latter colors. In all, Wedgwood introduced eight patterns in underglaze (1805-1810), which included the famous peony and botanical flowers patterns.

Pearl Ware

To compete in the growing porcelain market, Wedgwood introduced Pearl Ware in 1779. Pearl, a variation on Queen's Ware, was modified with added white clay and flint, as well as a small amount of cobalt oxide further whitening the appearance. This resulted in a whiter surface with an almost undetectable hint of blue sheen from the additional blue oxide coloring.

Surprisingly, Pearl did not remain in production for very long. Though attractive, Pearl always had the slightly blue pearl essence characteristic that did not catch on as the white Creamware did. Thus, Pearl never reached the same acclaim as the Creamware, which the public considered more attractive. In addition, to make production of Pearl Ware worthwhile for Wedgwood, an entire factory would have been needed to produce Pearl in large enough quantities. Wedgwood produced Pearl sporadically until about 1940, using it for particular projects such as their shell and nautical shaped pieces. Wedgwood's Bone China, which had been growing in popularity, eventually took the lead of Pearl Ware competing in the porcelain market. Bone China was closer in composition and manufacturing methods to the wares coming out of China and could stand up better to the Chinese-styled shapes and decoration that the public demanded.

Stained Creamware

In 1858, Wedgwood created a stained Creamware named Celadon, imitating an old eighteenth century Chinese pottery style. Celadon began as a glaze of varying shades of green, used in some Chinese Stoneware of the Sung Dynasty (960-1280). In the eighteenth century, the Chinese used a similar color as a ground for their porcelain. Additional stains by Wedgwood included a lavender color introduced about the same time, honey buff in 1930, Windsor grey 1953, and cane in 1957. Celadon later appeared briefly on Bone China in 1882. Other stained items existed in Wedgwood's long list of experiments with different potting techniques and decorations, depending on their style and purpose, such as Drab Queen's Ware and Alpine Pink Bone China.

Pearl Ware "Pap Feeder," c. 1810. Half-covered and decorated with Oriental motif in transfer print. The funnel shaped spout was used by a parent to feed liquid to an ill child. *Courtesy of the Slavid Collection.* $250-300.

White Ware

White Ware was an earthenware pottery that was a cross between Creamware and Porcelain, incorporating characteristics of both. Wedgwood introduced White Ware in 1805 to compete with the imported Chinese Porcelain flowing into England at the time. Josiah Wedgwood II had enjoyed some success with Pearl Ware in trying to capture the market for whiter wares, but his development of Bone China had not yet been perfected. The White Ware acted as an intermediate step towards competing in the porcelain-dominated market for whiter-than-white wares.

White Ware's chemical composition closely resembled earthenware clay, but with added china clay and it was also fired at higher temperatures than Queen's Ware or Pearl Ware. White Ware filled the gap between Creamware and the consumer migration toward various types of porcelains. It was whiter than Pearl Ware, but not as delicate or refined as the Bone China wares that would come after it. White Ware was used for tea wares to compete with porcelain, but found its calling in an altogether different area. A slightly thicker version of white ware was found to be very durable and suitable for Chamber Ware, sometimes referred to as "Toilet Ware."

White Ware bidet in wooden frame and cover, c. early 1800s. *Courtesy of the Frazier Collection.* $700-800.

Chamber Ware

In the 1800s, indoor plumbing was non-existent. Instead, most hygienic needs were satisfied using Chamber Ware items. These included utilitarian items like chamber pots, washing bowls, water jugs, soap dishes, soapboxes, slop pails, and basins. White Ware offered a very sanitary, clean white appearance. Eighteenth century Chamber Ware items were smaller than later versions as they were often concealed in special cupboards. Chamber Ware was discontinued prior to 1896.

Ceramic Printing Company — Sadler & Green

John Sadler and Guy Green were well known in the 1750s for their work with transfer printing on Creamware plates, tiles, and other shapes. Sadler & Green, as the firm was known, had adapted traditional transfer printing methods and utilized a system where they could turn out inexpensively printed products at a high rate for potteries such as Wedgwood.

Sadler & Green were contracted to perform transfer-printing work for Wedgwood, however Wedgwood was concerned that their competitors would soon discover Sadler & Green. In 1761, Wedgwood loaded Sadler & Green with orders to fill their production capacity, thus preventing them from having time to produce printed wares for other competing potteries. Sadler & Green's work with Wedgwood continued until sometime after Josiah Wedgwood passed away in 1795.

Husk Service & Frog Service

Two of the most famous of Wedgwood's Queen's Ware services were made for Catherine the Great of Russia: the Husk Service and the Frog Service. The Husk was a simple tea service, decorated with rose-purple borders of husk festoons and botanical flowers. Catherine the Great was so taken with the new Wedgwood service that she commissioned the Frog Service.

The Frog Service was named for the palace she was having built at Kekereski, also known as *La Grenouilliere* (the frog marsh). Each piece was adorned with laurel leaves and a crest with an image of a frog. While Wedgwood was concerned about being paid for the service, the returns to Wedgwood in recognition and reputation far exceeded the costs of materials and labor efforts. Wedgwood completed the service in 1775 at an approximate base cost of £3,000 English pounds. This was the largest, single most costly dinner service ever to come out of England. In all, the service contained 952 pieces. The pieces were decorated with 1,244 different hand-painted images depicting actual scenes from around Great Britain.

Plate from the Husk Service of Catherine the Great of Russia, c. 1770. *Courtesy of the Chellis and Adams Collection.* $600-800.

Today, pieces from the Husk Service and Frog Service are very scarce. Only a few of the Frog pieces are in private or museum collections, the remaining items are

Plate, c. late 1700s. Feather edged with Rococo style molded rose center. Originally feather edge gilded, a trace of gold still left. Black transfer printing of exotic birds, six on flange and a trio on the molded rose center. Transfer printed by Sadler & Green of Liverpool. Not marked, 8.5". *Courtesy of the Dorothy Lee-Jones Collection.* $230-270.

in the Hermitage Museum in Russia. Valuing pieces such as these is extremely difficult, as they rarely ever come up at auction. The last known piece was a dessert-sized Frog Service plate, which sold for nearly $20,000 at Skinner's Auction House in Boston, Massachusetts.

In 1995, for the Bicentennial of Josiah Wedgwood's death, Wedgwood released Frog Service reproductions. These included five different shapes and scenes, and production numbered 3,000 of each design. The subjects were of Etruria Hall on an oval dish, and four desert plates depicting Earl Gower's Park, Kew Gardens, Wilton Castle, and Wimpole. In 1995, their cost was $75 for the oval plate and $39 for each dessert-sized plate. Shortly after their release, these replicas easily tripled in value. Wedgwood also produced another run of similar commemoratives in 1998 as part of the Genius Collection. They produced these in greater number, 10,000 pieces per design, and they appear occasionally in the on-line auction sites today.

Retailer: Jones, McDuffee & Stratton, Co.

One of the most important ceramic retailers in the American market for Wedgwood was Jones, McDuffee & Stratton, Co. (JM&S). In the mid-1800s, JM&S was the largest importer of pottery, porcelain, and glass in the United States. Their business dealings with Wedgwood helped expand the growing interest and demand for Wedgwood products in the growing American market. What developed between the two companies was a collaborative effort to cater to the American consumer's ceramic needs and sensibilities. Some Wedgwood collectors today take special interest in Commemorative Wares that were sold through JM&S during the 1800s and 1900s. A few of the collectable and Commemorative Wares that were distributed through JM&S were the Old Blue Historical Plates, calendar tiles, and the Piranesi plates

Old Blue Historical Plates

In addition to the importation and sale of wares that Wedgwood produced during this time, specific signature runs of products have become synonymous with the Jones McDuffee & Stratton, Co. name. Perhaps the best known product line to come out of the JM&S / Wedgwood affiliation was the Old Blue Historical plates. These plates celebrated various American subjects in blue transfer print on Wedgwood's Creamware, images included various American colleges, historical monuments, famous naval vessels, and the forefathers of the American Revolution. Wedgwood introduced the first thirty-five plates in 1899; these would be followed by many more over the decades, covering a thousand different subjects.

Calendar Tiles

Another interesting series of Wedgwood collectables, frequently associated with the JM&S name are calendar tiles, produced between 1879-1929. Calendar tiles are rectangular shaped Creamware tiles that Wedgwood produced as give-away samples for JM&S clients. They were similar to the Old Blue Historical plates in decoration, as they depicted mostly themes and places from around Boston and Cambridge, Massachusetts, though not exclusively. They created about fifty different scenes. Some tiles in fact shared the same images as the Old Blue Historical plates. One example, pictured in this book, depicts the U.S.S. Constitution under sail. The tile and plate share near identical scenes.

The calendar tiles were commonly made with brown-transfer print on a 3" x 4" Creamware tile. A number of these subjects can also be found printed in gray, blue gray, blue, light brown, green, the 1879 example is purple, and in the case of the 1896 tile, polychrome. Most tiles include a calendar year printed on one-side and an image on the other. A few have no calendar on the reverse side, only a potters stamp or even blank. Most tiles are pierced at either the top or side depending on the vertical or horizontal orientation of the image. These holes were intended for use in hanging the tile for display.

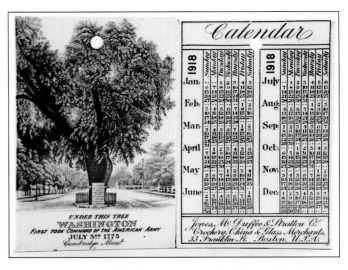

Two calendar tiles, 1899. Scene depicting the *Tree under which Washington took command* in brown transfer print, 4.75". The other tile has the backside facing with the calendar for 1918 (Boston Light). *Author's Collection.* $90-110 each.

Most of the tiles were made for the American market with a few exceptions; one example is the 1887 tile depicting the S.S. *Britannia* and S.S. *Etruria* which was done for Grover Harrison China Hall of Toronto, Canada. The official markings on all these tiles began in 1917 with "WEDGWOOD ETRURIA ENGLAND" printed on the side of the tile. Although the earlier tiles did not include Wedgwood markings, they usually included "Jones, McDuffee & Stratton, Co." printed on the calendar side of the tile.

There is also a little know tile with the 1882 calendar on one side and the Bonner's Map of Boston, Massachusetts, as depicted on the 1885 tile. No explanation has ever surfaced, nor has anything been written about this anomaly. It has been suggested that this may have been a prototype tile, not intended for distribution. The avid calendar tile enthusiast may come across an occasional oddity that does not fit in the before mentioned categories. The web site, www.antiquecalendar. com/tiles, notes that there have been additional tiles made for retailers other than JM&S. Some of these subjects include The Atheneum – St. Johnsbury, Vermont, and the Hannah Duston Monument – Haverhill, Massachusetts.

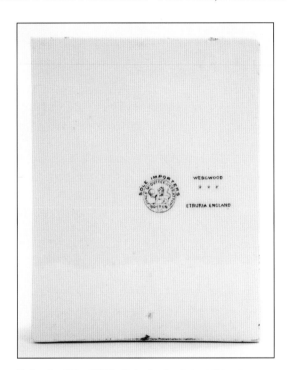

Calendar Tile, 1922. Only the back is visible; the back is without calendar and instead has a Jones, McDuffee & Stratton marking and a Wedgwood stamp. The front depicts *The Cathedral Church of St. Paul* in brown transfer print, 4.25". *Author's Collection.* $90-110.

Piranesi Plates

The Piranesi plates were a series of plates decorated with designs by Giovanni Battista Piranesi (1720-1778), an Italian Engraver who specialized in architectural drawings. In 1958, Wedgwood produced a series of plates using Piranesi's images on Creamware dinner plates in the Edme style (a round plate design with a ribbed boarded around the edge). Archbishop Richard J. Cushing of Boston, Massachusetts, had commissioned this set, depicting architectural views of Rome. Each plate includes a description of the scene on the back of the plate and marked with Wedgwood and Jones McDuffee & Stratton stamps.

Queen's Ware Artists

Artist: Emile Lessore

To speak of Wedgwood artists and their contributions to the history of Queen's Ware, it is essential to mention Emile Lessore and his work. Lessore was a freelance artist who took Wedgwood tableware shapes and transformed them into hand-painted works of art. Lessore utilized Wedgwood's Queen's Ware table shapes as canvas for his intricate and decorative one-of-a-kind illustrations. His works are highly valued and rare treasures to today's Wedgwood collector.

Lessore was a French painter, engraver, and ceramic artist who came to England in 1858 to escape the grief he experienced upon the death of his wife. He went to Wedgwood, based on the company's reputation as the leader in the pottery trade. There he was afforded a workspace in Wedgwood's factory and given free-reign to pursue his own work and design ideas. He asked to be left on his own and in turn Wedgwood would not be required to pay for any of his creations of which they did not approve. Lessore agreed to pay for any materials he used, and would keep for his own purposes any items that Wedgwood did not wish to purchase. He remained in England for five years, most of which was spent at Wedgwood's Etruria factory. He left England in 1863 due to health reasons and returned home to France where he continued his work for Wedgwood for several more years until his death in 1876.

Plate, c. 1865. Spanish shape, Aesop Fables design, hand-painted by Emile Lessore, signed "E. Lessore." *Courtesy of the Chellis and Adams Collection.* $650-750.

19

In the 1840s, Wedgwood was recovering from a financial slump and had not yet recovered artistically in their production lines. Wedgwood had been struggling for several years against a growing competitor, Minton (founded by Thomas Minton), which had taken a portion of its market share. Lessore's arrival was a welcomed change that helped steer the company in new artistic directions. Lessore brought back to Wedgwood a revived sense of art and individual creativity.

As mentioned, Lessore's work for Wedgwood mainly involved hand-painted designs on Queen's Ware tableware shapes, plaques, and tablets. His art has been described as impressionistic in style. His subjects were typically romantic scenes or peaceful scenes of children at play. He also produced dreamy landscape scenes and a few religious images of Christ as well as Greek mythological figures. For his relatively few years at Wedgwood, and several free-lancing years afterward, he managed to produce a variety of intricate and exceptional works of art on various Queen's Ware shapes. Each piece was individually hand-painted, never mass-produced.

Two Ivanhoe pattern pieces by Thomas Allen, 1906. (Left) Hexagon shaped pitcher, green print (DEI mark), (right) short creamer, blue print with "Ivanhoe" printed on the front (AHI mark). *Courtesy of the Rosen Collection.* (Left) $75-90, (right) $70-85.

Lessore's wares were numerous for one artist, but for today's collector his creations are somewhat rare finds. Those lucky enough to find a Lessore piece often pay high prices even for the smallest pieces. Some of Lessore's work that is more elaborate can command high prices into the thousands for a single piece.

Artist: Thomas Allen

Thomas Allen was an artist, brought in to Wedgwood in 1876 to replace the loss of Emile Lessore. He came over from Minton and worked with tableware and some hand-painted vases. When he was promoted to Art Director in 1878, his time was split between overseeing other Wedgwood painters and designers and designing scenes for transfer-printed Creamware. Allen retired in 1904.

One of his more famous designs was his adaptation of *Ivanhoe*, from the story of the same name by Sir Walter Scott. The story took place during the time of King Richard the Lion-Hearted where Ivanhoe was a medieval Crusader, returning home from war. His pursuit was to reclaim his family's land and he encounters various famous characters from the period, including Robin Hood. Thomas Allen also produced a series of over-sized round plaques that he hand-painted colorful portraits on. The subjects were characters taken from various works of Shakespeare.

Artist/Potter: Victor Skellern

Skellern had the distinction of becoming Wedgwood's first educated and professionally trained Art Director in 1934 after graduating from the Royal College of Art (Skellern was later promoted to Head of Design for Wedgwood). Skellern made numerous contributions to Wedgwood tableware shapes and designs. In 1964, Skellern created a special collectable to honor the 400th anniversary of William Shakespeare's birth. The piece was a tankard painted with scenes taken from twelve famous Shakespearean plays. In addition to the tankard, the celebratory collection included a reissue of Hackwood's 1777 Shakespeare portrait medallion and a reissue of a Shakespeare bust copied from a Wedgwood black Basalt bust from 1774.

Artist: Clare Leighton

Clare Veronica Hope Leighton (Wedgwood: 1898-1989) was a painter, wood-engraver, and author who produced several freelance designs for Wedgwood. She is best known in Wedgwood collecting circles for her series of twelve Wedgwood plates done in 1951, illustrating various scenes of New England industries. The plates were made of Queen's Ware with intricate illustrations in black colored transfer print. The industries represented include Whaling, Cod Fishing, Lobster Fishing, Ice Cutting, Sugaring, Shipbuilding, Grist Milling, Logging, Cranberrying, Marble Quarrying, Farming, and Tobacco Growing. Clare Leighton later produced a four-plate series on views of the Taft School.

Plate with black transfer print, 1952. Depicting *Lobstering* from the New England Industries series, designed by Clare Leighton, 10.5". *Author's Collection.* $60-75.

Artist/Potter: Eric Ravilious

Eric Ravilious was another freelance artist who worked for Wedgwood. He had known Victor Skellern, Wedgwood's Head of Design, from the Royal College of Art. It was Skellern who suggested that Wedgwood examine Ravilious' work. Ravilious then went on to produce sophisticated designs for use on Queen's Ware table shapes including plates, bowls, and mugs. Some of his earliest designs were his commemorative pieces for the Coronation of King Edward VIII in 1935, which Wedgwood later reused with minor changes for the coronations of King George VI in 1937 and Queen Elizabeth II in 1953. They were produced again in 2002 to commemorate the 50th anniversary of Queen Elizabeth II's accession to the throne.

The designs by Ravilious were originally intended for the traditional method of transfer printing, involving engraving on reverse molds then transferring the image onto the subject shape. Interestingly, a new innovation of lithographically transferring drawings started at Wedgwood during Ravilious' time. This production change led to occasional color deviations from Ravilious' original designs. Long after Ravilious had left, the company produced his designs in a number of different combinations.

Ravilious' designs appear on a number of classic Wedgwood shapes by potters Norman Wilson and Victor Skellern including the famous *Barlaston Mug*, which was made specifically for Eric Ravilious to decorate. The *Barlaston Mug* was designed to mark the opening of the new Barlaston, England, factory for Wedgwood in 1940. The only known shape that was designed by Ravilious himself was a tea set preserve jar.

Several pieces that Ravilious' decorated are the *Harvest Festival* (a.k.a. Persephone) and *Troy* patterns introduced in 1936; *Alphabet* nursery ware *Afternoon Tea*, introduced in 1937; *Travel, Boat Race Day,* and *Garden* patterns in 1938; *Garden Implements, Noel,* the *Four Continents Bowl,* and the *London Underground Plate* introduced in 1939.

The works produced by Eric Ravilious for Wedgwood were complex, yet brief in quantity due to the events of World War II. Ravilious left Wedgwood to serve in the Royal Marines and was killed in the line of duty in 1942.

Creamer, c. 1937. Decorated with "Alphabet" pattern by Eric Ravilious. *Courtesy of the Slavid Collection.* $300-350.

Artist: Margaret Philbrick

Margaret Philbrick was a freelance artist who designed a number of scenes for Wedgwood tableware. Beginning in 1899 with the Old Blue Historical plates, the market was fascinated with intricate tableware designs. Numerous Wedgwood artists and freelance artists such as Philbrick were pressed into service to generate a continuous supply of scenes depicting colleges, universities, historical figures and places, famous ships, and architecture even into the mid-1900s.

Margaret Philbrick was actually in the employment of Jones McDuffee & Stratton, Co. from 1944-1955. Jones McDuffee & Stratton, Co. would provide Philbrick with photographs or descriptions of designs and borders that they needed. Philbrick then created pencil drawings in the size and shape in which the design would fit on the plate. This required fine detailed work to include all the appropriate details in such a confined space. Jones McDuffee & Stratton, Co. then shipped her drawings to England where Wedgwood engravers would prepare copperplate engravings of the drawings for printing onto the plates.

Not all of Philbrick's work was limited to the Old Blue Historical type work. She also used the largest tableware piece as one of her designs, a 19" Creamware platter depicting the U.S. Military Academy at West Point. Some of her other work included a number of colleges and universities, usually in the New England area, plus some nautical designs for a series of plates made for the Peabody Museum.

Oval platter, c. 1950. Creamware with red transfer print, depicting an aerial view of West Point Academy by Margaret Philbrick. This piece was autographed by Philbrick on the reverse. 18 5/8". *Courtesy of the Frazier Collection.* $600-800.

Oval plate from the Frog Service of Catherine the Great of Russia, 1775. The scene depicted is thought to be the Earl of Stamford Estate, with border decorations of oak leaves and acorns. There is a crest at the top with a green frog symbolizing the palace she was having built at Kekereski, also known as *La Grenouilliere* (the frog marsh). (WEDGWOOD mark and 311 mark). *Courtesy of the Chellis and Adams Collection.* $35,000-45,000.

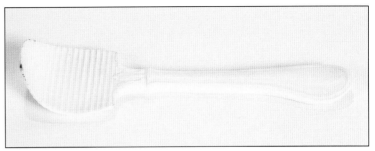

Butter scoop, c. 1790, 6.25". *Courtesy of the Slavid Collection.* $200-300.

Tea canister, c. 1780. Features scene depicting *The Tea Party and the Good Shepherd. Courtesy of the Chellis and Adams Collection.* $300-450.

Oil & vinegar bottles with tray, c. late 1700s. *Courtesy of the Chellis and Adams Collection.* $400-550.

Creamware eggbeater, c. 1802. This eggbeater is in two parts with cutting spikes around the interior. It is a very rare to find these type pieces with all the spikes present and unbroken. *Courtesy of the Chellis and Adams Collection.* $500-550.

Pearl Ware flask, c. 1779. Flower sprigs in blue underglaze painted designs and "R. Wedgwood" printed on one side. It also has applied relief of bows and wreaths. This was possibly made for or by one of Josiah's relatives, perhaps Ralph Wedgwood. *Courtesy of the Chellis and Adams Collection.* $350-450.

Coffee pot and warmer, a.k.a. Veilleuse, c. 1785. *Courtesy
of the Chellis and Adams Collection.* $1,000-1,300.

Soup bowl, c. 1791. With royal crest printed in the center, 9.75".
Courtesy of the Chellis and Adams Collection. $100-110.

Molded ornament or "blancmange"
mold, c. late 1700s. Scallop molded,
4.75". *Courtesy of the Slavid Collection.*
$350-400.

Cup and saucer, c. 1785. Shell edge design with transfer printed exotic birds, printed for Wedgwood by Sadler & Green, Liverpool, (impressed Wedgwood mark). *Courtesy of the Dorothy Lee-Jones Collection*. $110-160.

Tureen stand, silver shape, c. late 1700s. Used as a base for a tureen, has molded surface to accept foot of tureen. Queen's Ware with a yellow tint glaze and polychrome enamels, raised feather edge with terra cotta enamel on the raised parts and mold handles. Floral wreathe in center with natural colored enamels, 16.25". *Courtesy of the Dorothy Lee-Jones Collection*. $285-315.

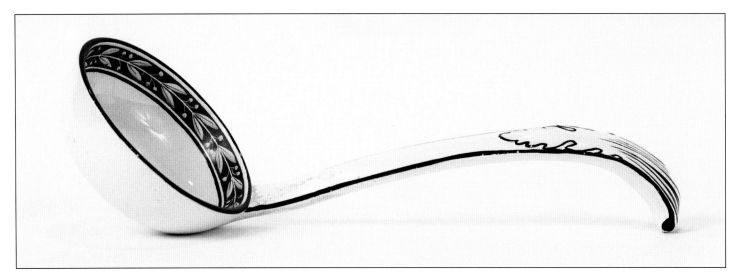

Ladle, c. 1790. Raspberry and black hand-painted highlighting, leaf and berries border. *Courtesy of the Horn and Hoffman Collection*. $250-450.

Hand-turned jug, c. 1786. Enameled in polychrome with a mounted cavalryman on one side and eagles on the other. *Courtesy of the Horn and Hoffman Collection*. $350-550.

Apothecary pill board, c. 1800. With measurement markings says, "Real Warranted Wedgwood" on the front. This was used for rolling and measuring pills with a scale for cutting them uniformly. 9.25" x 7.25". *Courtesy of the Rosen Collection.* $200-240.

Jelly mold with horse figure design, c. 1800, 5.25".
Courtesy of the Slavid Collection. $500-600.

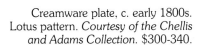

Creamware plate, c. early 1800s.
Lotus pattern. *Courtesy of the Chellis
and Adams Collection*. $300-340.

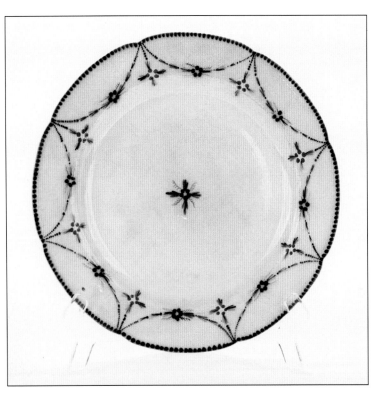

Pearl Ware plate, c. 1800s. Slight scalloped
edge, 9.5". *Courtesy of the Chellis and
Adams Collection*. $160-190.

Tile, c. 1800s. Depicting Josiah Wedgwood image and text that reads "Father of English Pottery," 9". *Courtesy of the Rosen Collection*. $300-350.

Toy sized tea cup and saucer, c. 1800s. Yellow glaze and olive green interior band on deep flange with five round dots, colored in thirds: black, yellow, brown. Cup and small saucer's design repeat on exterior of cup with yellow interior, cup 1.5" and saucer 3.5". *Courtesy of the Dorothy Lee-Jones Collection*. $300-325.

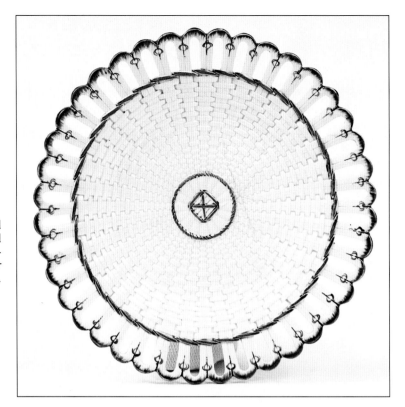

Pearl Ware plate, c. 1770-1780. Raised basket wave, Onion Pattern, and reticulated edge, blue enamel decoration, 9.25". *Courtesy of the Frazier Collection*. $600-650.

Pearl Ware plate, 1808-1809. Rare from the Botanical Flowers series. Illustrated in Coysh's blue transfer earthenware. *Courtesy of the Rosen Collection*. $340-390.

Coffee pot, c. early 1800s. Free-hand painted, green festoons and red dot trim. *Courtesy of the Horn and Hoffman Collection*. $400-500.

Pearl Ware plate, 1811. Water Lilly pattern in blue underglaze print, first made in 1808 with brown print, then blue 1811. *Courtesy of the Chellis and Adams Collection.* $300-400.

Octagon shaped dessert plate, c. 1812-1820. Old Man in the Mountain scene in the center in brown transfer print, 8". *Author's Collection.* $70-90.

Three Old Man of the Mountain Franconia Notch, New Hampshire, design pieces, c. 1812-1820.
(Left) Large creamer with green print, $100-120. (Center) Small creamer with blue print, $75-100.
(Right) Pitcher, hexagon shaped with green print, $90-110. *Courtesy of the Rosen Collection.*

Pearl Ware dessert plate, c. 1815. Multiple patterns engraved over each other. Peony pattern engraved design, probably by William Hales (1790-1815), blue hibiscus 1806-1808, water lily 1806. (Wedgwood under glaze mark), 8.5". *Courtesy of the Dorothy Lee-Jones Collection.* $380-430.

Dessert plate, c. 1815. White Ware with chrysanthemum pattern (a.k.a. Cryxa) printed in brown and enameled in iron-red, green, and cobalt with gilding. Pattern was first introduced in 1808, (Wedgwood impressed mark under glaze), 8". *Courtesy of the Dorothy Lee-Jones Collection.* $200-300.

Coffee can, teacup, and tea bowl-style saucer, c. 1815. Japanese style decoration, copied from Derby porcelain pattern late eighteenth century of Imari floras and colors with gold rim and gold on handles. Tea wares in this early date came with one saucer to service both cups. The saucer was usually deep. *Courtesy of the Dorothy Lee-Jones Collection.* $500-600.

White Ware plate (dessert-ware), c. 1840-1868. Apple green ground with hollyhock spray of three in grey and black transfer, gilded highlights, brown edge. (Pearl mark, printed: "Hollyhock.") 9.375". *Courtesy of the Dorothy Lee-Jones Collection.* $210-230.

Group of five different shapes hand-painted by Emile Lessore. *Courtesy of the Horn and Hoffman Collection.* (From left to right) Oval dish, scene with three children, signed "E. Lessore," c. 1860s, $300-400. Covered pot with two handles, signed "E. Lessore," c. 1860s, $400-500. Plate with Spanish shaped edges and painted scene of cupids playing, signed "E. Lessore," c. 1865, $450-550. Three-footed, covered pot with a picnic scene, signed "E. Lessore," c. 1870, $600-800. Diamond-shaped dish, scene of women working in the field, signed "E. Lessore," c. 1860s, $400-500.

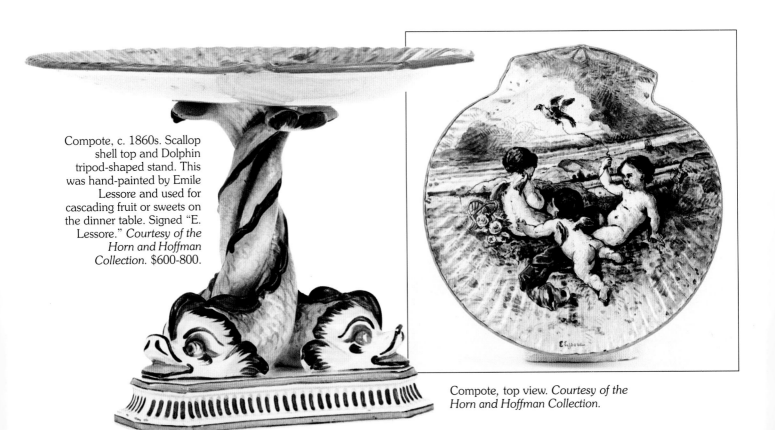

Compote, c. 1860s. Scallop shell top and Dolphin tripod-shaped stand. This was hand-painted by Emile Lessore and used for cascading fruit or sweets on the dinner table. Signed "E. Lessore." *Courtesy of the Horn and Hoffman Collection.* $600-800.

Compote, top view. *Courtesy of the Horn and Hoffman Collection.*

Scallop shell plate, c. 1860s. Decoration depicting two cupids hand-painted by Emile
Lessore, signed "E. Lessore." *Courtesy of the Horn and Hoffman Collection.* $400-500.

Oval Dish, 1863. Hand-painted design by Emile Lessore in the Watteau, Fragonard or Boucher style, (TII mark). 3.375". *Courtesy of the Frazier Collection.* $300-350.

Three plates in the Spanish shape. By Emile Lessore from the Aesop Fables series, each signed "E. Lessore." (Left) fall scene (FNU mark), 1866, (center) plate with wolf in center (FOX mark), 1869, and (right) bridge over water (FOP mark), 1861. *Courtesy of the Chellis and Adams Collection.* $800-1,000 each.

Table Center, c. 1860s. Creamware by Emile Lessore. Consists of
an oval dish with pierced edges supported by horse figures.
Courtesy of the Chellis and Adams Collection. $4,500-6,500.

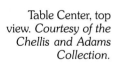Table Center, top
view. *Courtesy of the
Chellis and Adams
Collection.*

Oil bottle or scent bottle, c. 1862. Hand-painted by Emile Lessore and signed: "E. Lessore." Roman wrestlers used bottles in this shape for oil. To wash off dirt after wrestling, they would apply oil to the body and remove it with a stick. The bottle has an extra piece that runs from the lip to the body, to help grip the piece when pouring. In later centuries the shape was adopted for scent bottles. *Courtesy of the Chellis and Adams Collection.* $500-600.

Pearl Ware plate, 1864. Reticulated edge, hand-painted turquoise highlighting around the edges and gold geometric pattern in the center, (Pearl, FHS marks), 8.75". *Author's Collection.* $300-350.

Lessore pitcher, c. 1860s. 4" x 6". Hole in center of top, top itself is 1.5" tall. *Courtesy of the Chellis and Adams Collection.* $550-700.

Vase, 1869. White Ware, of a classic Chinese shape, with two molded dog or stylized human flattened faces surrounded by a .5" ring. (ODX mark), 7.5". *Courtesy of the Dorothy Lee-Jones Collection.* $280-320.

Tile, c. 1875. From a set of twelve, Japanese subjects painted in Mikado-style with diaper patterned background, 8". *Courtesy of the Horn and Hoffman Collection.* $150-200.

Plant stand, c. mid-1800s. Hand-painted enamel floral designs. Stands 3' tall and is hollow. *Courtesy of the Chellis and Adams Collection.* $800-1,100.

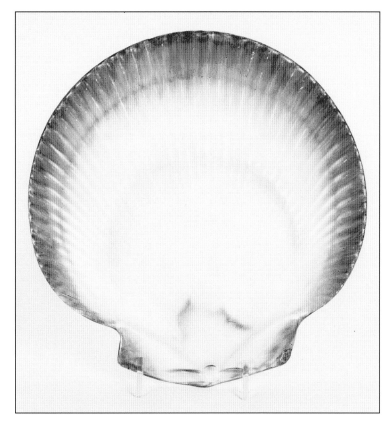

Pearl Ware shell plate, c. 1870. From the "Nautilus
WEDGWOOD Service," "Pecten Japonicum plate."
Courtesy of the Frazier Collection. $125-175.

Teapot, c. 1874.
Satsuma shape,
decorated in the Imari
style, enameled and
gilded. (Wedgwood
under glaze mark,
pattern C1337 13).
*Courtesy of the
Dorothy Lee-Jones
Collection.* $450-550.

Tile, c. 1875-1902. Blue transfer print scene depicting the Wadsworth Longfellow House, Portland, Maine, 6". *Author's Collection.* $150-200.

Plate, 1876-1883. In the Edinburgh style, design by Thomas Allen, 8.25". *Courtesy of the Frazier Collection.* $45-75.

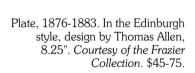

Charger, 1877. Hand-painted picture of an old person, reverse side reads "Souvenir de Rembrandt after H. Herkomer ARA F. RHEAD." The piece was hand-painted and signed by artist Fredrick A. Rhead, (DGF mark), 12.125". *Courtesy of the Horn and Hoffman Collection.* $600-800.

Pitcher, 1876. One of the oldest Commemorative Ware pieces made. Celebrates the American Centennial in 1876. (EFC mark) *Courtesy of the Rosen Collection.* $300-350.

Tile, c. 1877-1890. Part of a set of 12, each for a different month, designed by Helen J. A. Miles. This particular tile has December printed on bottom right and a hand-painted Christmas scene of a boy and girl under mistletoe. *Courtesy of the Chellis and Adams Collection.* $100-130.

Large vase, 1877. Features a tile-like design on front, of the month of December. Month design by Helen J. A. Miles (COF mark), 11". *Courtesy of the Rosen Collection.* $300-350.

Pearl Ware plate, 1877. Basket weave pattern A4049 and Chinese designs over glaze (AKF mark). *Courtesy of the Horn and Hoffman Collection.* $150-200.

Tile, c. 1878. "Mustard" design on front from the "Midsummer Night's Dream" series by Helen J. A. Miles. *Courtesy of the Slavid Collection.* $110-130.

Botanical bowl, 1878. (TPG mark), 11". *Courtesy of the Frazier Collection.* $80-150.

Plate, c. 1900s. Brown transfer print with "Devil Fish" design. Medieval border from the "Fish and Boys" series (originally for a set of tiles c. 1880-1883). *Courtesy of the Rosen Collection.* $150-300.

Longfellow Jug, c. 1880. Transfer printed. This was a presentation piece to poet Henry Wadsworth Longfellow. The image of Longfellow on the front was reproduced from a photo by George W. Rhead. On the back of the jug are a few lines from the poem "Keramos." *Courtesy of the Frazier Collection.* $400-500.

Plate, c. 1880. Red border and hand-painted scene depicting cows in a pond. This was probably painted after it left the factory, 10". *Courtesy of the Frazier Collection*. $125-175.

Plate, 1881. Japanese Geisha design in the style of "Mikado," from a series of twelve enameled subjects first produced in 1871 and later reused on tiles, (3AJ mark), 10.25". *Courtesy of the Frazier Collection*. $75-150.

Pearl Ware vase, 1886. Imari (Japanese) style, (3DO mark). The Imari style is driven by a two-color mix, in this case with blue underglaze and dark red, decorated with Japanese flowers. This was part of Wedgwood's "Japan Patterns" that became popular after the International Exhibition in London in 1862, 9.25". *Courtesy of the Frazier Collection*. $150-200.

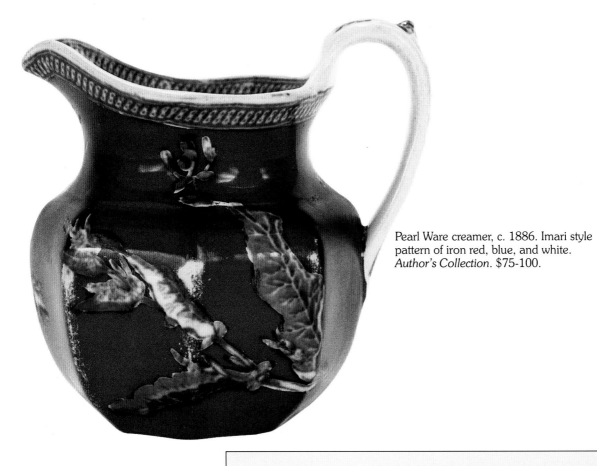

Pearl Ware creamer, c. 1886. Imari style pattern of iron red, blue, and white. *Author's Collection*. $75-100.

Pearl Ware spirit (Whiskey) barrel, c. 1890. Missing spigot. *Courtesy of the Frazier Collection*. $250-300.

Plate, 1890. Japanese design and Basket Pattern, (JMS mark),
9". *Courtesy of the Frazier Collection.* $50-75.

Plate with green border, 1905. Says "more rain more rest, fair weather isn't always best." Jolly pattern indicated on back, from the Fisherman Series by John Leech first issued on tiles 1880-1883, then on plates 1905. *Courtesy of the Rosen Collection.* $200-250.

Plate with green border that says, "Life's a grind & woman's unkind. The wind in the east & man's a beast." From the Fisherman Series after John Leech, first issued on tiles in 1880-1883, then on plates. 10", 1891. *Courtesy of the Chellis and Adams Collection.* $200-250.

Platter, 1892. Blue Landscape pattern with rose border, 12 3/8"
x 9.25". *Courtesy of the Frazier Collection.* $125-150.

Tea canister, c. late 1800s. With dome
cover, knob finial, and iron red and black
enameled decoration. An eighteenth
century style but revived in a nineteenth
century look. Manufactured for James
Powell & Sons, White Friars Glass Works,
London, 2.75". *Courtesy of the Dorothy
Lee-Jones Collection.* $160-220.

Creamware "Liverpool" shaped jug, c. 1895. Image depicting the
America's Cup Yacht, the *Intrepid*, designed by Robert Center in 1878,
10.5". *Courtesy of the Donald Eric Johnson Collection.* $500-700.

Plate, c. 1800s. Creamware, diamond shaped. 11" x 11.5". "EC" monogram in center. *Courtesy of the Chellis and Adams Collection.* $150-180.

Two-handled dish, c. late 1800s. Applied foliate slip decoration by Harry Barnard. *Courtesy of the Chellis and Adams Collection.* $400-500.

Three Fairbanks House pieces in blue transfer print, *Courtesy of the Frazier Collection.* (Left) Plate, 1912. Depicting on front the *Fairbanks Family in America Settled 1636 in Dedham Mass*, (3JO mark), 9.25", $50-75. (Center) Tile, c. 1904. Depicting image of the Fairbanks House design, 6", $100-125. (Right) Plate, c. 1904. Depicting an image of the Fairbanks House design, 9.25", $75-100.

Plate, c. 1887. Raised fan motif around edge, hand-painted Oriental Geisha design in center (Wedgwood mark in red, underglaze). *Courtesy of the Horn and Hoffman Collection.* $150-200.

Blue/Green/Yellow and Olive/Yellow on Queens Ware medallions, c. 1800s. Zephyrs relief, unmarked, except for color information etched in script on the reverse. Most likely Wedgwood. These were no doubt trial pieces. 2" x 3". *Courtesy of the Chellis and Adams Collection.* Each: $105-130.

Plate, c. early 1900s. Design from Ivanhoe pattern by Thomas Allen. *Courtesy of the Rosen Collection.* $75-120.

Hot milk jug from a Dejuener set, c. early 1800s. Dome shaped cover with small ball finial. Decorated with pink lustre bands, green leaves, terra cotta colors, and half flowers. Reminiscent of Gaudy Welsh style (without the blue coloring), 5.5" x 3.25". *Courtesy of the Dorothy Lee-Jones Collection*. $300-450.

Pair of Custard cups or ice cups, c. 1996. Reproductions from the Catherine the Great Frog Service. Part of the Genius Collection, limited edition of 4,000. (Left) Scene depicts views at Richmond and of a Ruined Castle, (right) scene depicts views on the Thames near London. *Author's Collection*. $50-75 each.

Vase with blue print, c. 1995. Depicting Windsor Castle, Berkshire, from the
"Romantic England" series, 12.5". *Courtesy of the Frazier Collection.* $80-100.

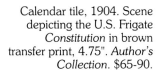

Slop pail with cover, c. 1900s. White Ware with Willow pattern in multi-colors, rattan handle. *Courtesy of the Rosen Collection.* $600-700.

Calendar tile, 1904. Scene depicting the U.S. Frigate *Constitution* in brown transfer print, 4.75". *Author's Collection.* $65-90.

The U.S. Frigate Constitution in Chase.
Also known as "Old Ironsides."
Launched at Boston. Oct 21. 1797.

Pearl Ware serving tray, c. 1900. Ivanhoe design, 14". *Courtesy of the Rosen Collection.* $180-215.

Three "Ivanhoe" pattern pieces by Thomas Allen, c. 1900-1906. (Left) Covered sugar, $60-80. (Center) Small side plate (TII mark), $50-60. (Right) Small jug with braided handle, $65-75. *Courtesy of the Rosen Collection.*

Bacchanalian jug, 1902. Enamel luster, (PLF), 7". *Courtesy of the Frazier Collection.* $130-150.

Platter inset in a metal tub, c. early 1900s. *Courtesy of the Rosen Collection.* $250-320.

"Mr. Punch" characters, 1903. Ivory glaze. Large platter, 17.5", $400-450,
Napier Jug with pewter top, $450-500. *Courtesy of the Rosen Collection.*

Cup and saucer, side plate,
1904. Black transfer print of
children. This series was made
for the French market. Pattern
#AM7392. Back reads
"Personages – Wedgwood
Etruria England import'*e*
D'Angleterre," (AQG mark).
*Courtesy of the Frazier
Collection.* $80-100.

Thomas Allan pieces from the "Banquet" series, 1903. Small dish is 3" and says "eaten bread is forgotten." Soup bowl says "enough, means health more – disease" (DPF mark). *Courtesy of the Rosen Collection.* Bowl: $100-140, Small dish: $50-75.

Plate, 1907. "Puck" design from A Midsummer Night's Dream series by Helen J. A. Miles, originally c. 1878, (3AJ mark), 10.5". *Courtesy of the Rosen Collection.* $100-110.

Playing Card motif designed by Augustus L. Jansson, 1910. Sectional tray: $400-500; creamer: $250-300. *Courtesy of the Rosen Collection.*

Canadian commemorative plates. (Left) Green border, "Toronto" (3CO mark), 1912. (Center) Orange border, "Dominion of Canada" (BZH mark), 1905. (Right) Blue border, "Winnipeg" (3DN mark), 1911. *Courtesy of the Rosen Collection.* $40-50 each.

Card jug, c. 1909. "Wedgwood Etruria England" and "copyright 1909 by Augustus T. Jameson West Somerville Mass" from the "Playing Card" series. *Courtesy of the Slavid Collection.* $350-400.

SYP Teapot (Simple Yet Perfect), 1911. Porcelain with blue printed Peony Pattern, 6" (3LN mark). *Courtesy of the Frazier Collection.* $350-450.

Octagonal-shaped jug, c. 1913. Hand-painted decoration in unknown Wedgwood design. This was part of a group of blank Queen's Ware shapes that Wedgwood shipped to local art schools for students to individually decorate as part of their training. The hand-painting is of lesser quality than that typically found on Wedgwood wares, indicating that is the work of an artist in training. (3FP mark), 4.5". *Courtesy of the Slavid Collection*. $300-400.

Toy dinner service, c. 1913. "Brownies" design by S. M. Daisy Makeig-Jones. Cambridge Ale shaped jug, 3.25", c. 1913, $250-350. Oval platter, 3.75", $300-400. *Courtesy of the Slavid Collection*.

Creamware cup, 1913. Registry mark an L, (3BP mark) and painted on
A481(7 or 4). Wedgwood Etruria stamped on with a "dsp" logo above it.
Courtesy of the Chellis and Adams Collection. $25-40.

Pearl Ware Lincoln plate, c. 1900s. Two of a kind. Beverly Rosen and her husband found the
engraving, never appearing to have been used in production. An employee of Wedgwood
then struck two of these, one for Wedgwood and one for the Rosens. This is the only full front
view of Lincoln, others have only been a profile or 3/4 views, ever to have been made by
Wedgwood. Features a circle mark. *Courtesy of the Rosen Collection.* $500-600.

Toy dinner and tea ware set, c. 1914.
Polychrome decoration Noah's Ark Pattern
by S. M. Daisy Makeig-Jones. *Courtesy of
the Slavid Collection.* $3,000-3,500.

Plate, 1916. Celadon color
stained-Creamware in the
Papillion Pattern by S. M.
Daisy Makeig-Jones. (3JS
mark). *Courtesy of the Frazier
Collection.* $225-275.

Cretan teapot and pair of cups and saucers, c. 1920. Designed by S. M. Daisy Makeig-Jones. The design consists
of classical warrior figures offset by a circular Celtic ornament in the front of each piece. Marked: "Cretan
Wedgwood Etruria England," impressed "Wedgwood." *Courtesy of the Slavid Collection.* $500-600.

Calendar tile, 1918. Scene depicting Boston Light in brown transfer print, 1918 calendar on reverse, 4.75". *Author's Collection.* $90-110.

Plate, c. 1920. Celtic ornaments in the Tyrone Pattern by S. M. Daisy Makeig-Jones enamel decoration beaded border. Tyrone is a county in Northern Ireland and the Tyrone Pattern is reminiscent of ancient Irish decorations of the region, 6.75". *Courtesy of the Slavid Collection.* $250-350.

Plate, c. 1920. Blue transfer print of the *Constitution*.
Courtesy of the Frazier Collection. $75-100.

Egg cup, c. 1920. Edme design. *Courtesy of the Frazier Collection*.
$50-80.

Orange Basket, 1920. Creamware with reticulated body (3QW mark) The Orange Basket resembles the Chestnut Basket style. The difference between the two is that the Orange has a reticulated bottom half; the Chestnut has a solid bottom half. *Courtesy of the Frazier Collection*. $ 350-450.

Dessert plate, 1922. Cornflower design with shell-edge. *Courtesy of the Frazier Collection.* $35-50.

Pitcher, c. 1923. Moa Pattern jug designed by S. M. Makeig-Jones for "Nursery Ware." Polychrome decoration with bird design. The Moa was a large, flightless bird from New Zealand that was hunted to extinction centuries ago, 5.25". *Courtesy of the Slavid Collection.* $700-900.

Dessert plate, 1927. From the Ferrara Tableware series with mulberry colored transfer print, (4QD mark), 8". *Author's Collection.* $30-60.

Plate, 1925. Black background and Chinoiserie design, (4YB mark). *Courtesy of the Frazier Collection.* $150-250.

Charger, 1930. This is considered the middle of three sizes of chargers decorated by
Alfred H. Powell. (4QF mark), 18 5/8". *Courtesy of the Slavid Collection.* $5,000.

Charger, c. 1930. Reverse side decorated with painted plant
leaves around the edges. *Courtesy of the Slavid Collection.*

Ash tray, c. 1930. Blue flowers, 4.25".
Courtesy of the Frazier Collection. $20-40.

Hunt jug, 1932. Blue glaze and hound shaped handle (Dye Ken John Peel stamp). *Author's Collection.* $120-150.

Two Evangeline plates, c. 1939. On back: "Meanwhile apart in the twilight gleem of a window's embrace sat the lovers." Purple printed plate, 8.75", $50-125. Blue printed plate, 8.75", $75-125. *Courtesy of the Frazier Collection.*

Two tableware pieces. Designed by Eric Ravilious. (Right) dish in the Persephone pattern, c. 1936, 9", $30-40. (Left) High rimmed dish in the Garden pattern, 1938, $20-25. *Author's Collection*.

Country Lovers figure, c. 1940. Modeled by Arnold Machin with some enamel decoration, 13". Unlike this figure, undecorated examples are of lesser value. *Courtesy of the Slavid Collection*. $1,200-1,800.

75

Taurus the Bull, c. 1945. Cast figure of a bull looking down towards the ground. It is covered with a black glossy glaze with Ravilious-style printed zodiac designs. Designed by Arnold Machin. *Courtesy of the Dorothy Lee-Jones Collection*. $600-800.

Large punch bowl, c. 1945. For Morgan & Co., of Montreal, commemorating an anniversary. Bottom reads, "Population 1845 45,000, Population 1945 1,500,000," inside of rim reads, "Discovered Jacques Cartier en 1534." *Courtesy of the Slavid Collection*. $400-500.

Plate, c. 1970s. Depicts the clipper ship, the *Union*.
Courtesy of the Chellis and Adams Collection. $50-75.

Plate, c. 1900s. Edme shape with "American University of Beirut" in center. *Courtesy of the Rosen Collection.* $65-80.

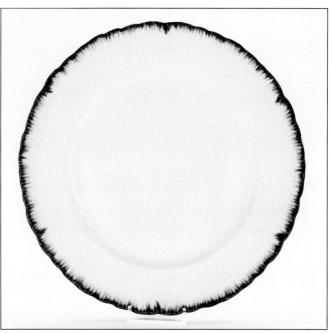

Shell edged plate, c. 1900s. Williamsburg reproduction. *Courtesy of the Frazier Collection.* $55-80.

Three small tumblers, c. 1950. Reproductions of originals in the Peabody Museum, made for the Peabody Museum. *Courtesy of the Frazier Collection*. Set: $75-100.

Monteith, 1953. Has the names of the original thirteen colonies on a chain-ring, with US Navy motto, "Sustentans et Sustentatum" Made for the 25th Anniversary of the Wedgwood Club, Boston. *Courtesy of the Frazier Collection*. $100-250.

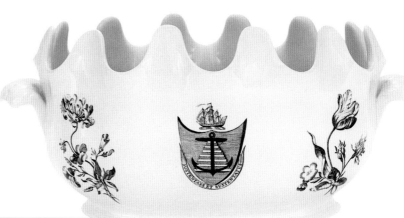

Four Embossed Queen's Ware items: Ash Tray, c. 1955, blue with white grapevine relief, $20-30. Vase in the Edme shape, c. 1979, with blue grape leaf border, 8.75", $110-130. Side Plate, c. 1949, white with pink grapevine relief, $25-50. Rope-handled jug, c. 1950, $125-150. *Courtesy of the Frazier Collection*.

Plate, c. 1950. The *Sooloo* ship from the Salem Series by Margaret Philbrick. The *Sooloo* was a wooden ship built in East Boston by John Taylor in 1861. Signed by Philbrick on reverse side, 10.5". *Courtesy of the Frazier Collection.* $25-45.

Three Piranesi plates, 1950. Brown transfer print, Edme shape, 10". Comes from a set of twelve, representing (left) the Barberini Palace, (center) interior of St. Paul outside the walls, (right) the castle at St. Angelo. *Author's Collection.* $40-60 each.

Plate 1959. "1759/1959" printed on front, special mark for Bicentenary year 1959, (6X59 mark, Wedgwood Barlaston circular stamp), 1075. *Courtesy of the Slavid Collection.* $350-450.

Dessert plate, c. 1980s. Reproduction of a Frog Service plate. *Courtesy of the Frazier Collection.* $75-80.

Plaque, c. 1990. Depicts the Clipper Ship, *Sea Witch*. Design reproduced from the original painting at the Peabody Museum. *Courtesy of the Frazier Collection.* $250-350.

Plate, 1960. Brown transfer print depicting the *Enterprise*
aircraft carrier, 11". *Author's Collection.* $30-45.

Ferrara Pattern group: platter, creamer, cup and saucer, soup cup, teapot, c. 1820s.
All featuring mulberry print. *Courtesy of the Frazier Collection.* Each: $50-250.

Chapter 3
Decorative Glazed Earthenware

Decorative glazed earthenware is a form that incorporates more thematic romanticism and fantasy, than Wedgwood's traditional classical approach. These wares are known for their shapes as well as their use of color as defining elements in artistic expression. This is particularly relevant to the mid-to-late nineteenth century when Victorian art was dominating the market. It illustrates Wedgwood's ability to keep their product line current with the trends of the market.

Majolica

Majolica, also known as art pottery, is a colorful Victorian-style glazed earthenware that dominated the decorative pottery market for most of the 1800s. Majolica is perhaps best known for its smooth and glossy finish, creative color patterns, and elaborate raised or molded designs. Majolica was not a Wedgwood innovation, but played an important role in Wedgwood's history.

The origins of Majolica can be traced back to Spanish tin-glazed earthenware in the thirteenth century, which bore very little resemblance to modern day Majolica. Tin-glazing derives its name from the addition of metallic tin-oxides to achieve a milky-white surface slip upon which colored glazes were added. During the fourteenth century, merchants brought these wares from Spain to Italy via the Isle of Majorca, a major port along the Mediterranean trade route. At that time, the name Majolica referred loosely to any ceramic that came through the Isle of Majorca, including these tin-glazed wares.

By the early fifteenth century, Italian potters were making their own tin-glazed ceramics called Maiolica. It was cheaper to make their own glazed wares than to import them from Spain. They used local reddish earthenware clays and coated them with a white opaque glaze made by mixing tin-ash into a cream-colored clay slip. The resulting white body would be colored in the desired design. The Italian potters had copied and improved on the imported wares, adapting Spanish techniques to their own artistic styles.

In 1850, Minton, a pottery company founded by Thomas Minton (a competitor of Wedgwood) developed what we know today as Majolica. Minton based his design loosely on the popular Italian colored wares, but reworked the manufacturing process and took his design in a more Victorian direction. Minton's new wares incorporated translucent, temperature-compatible glazes that formed a smooth, brilliantly colored glossy finish. Minton's new formulas and methods reduced crackling and offered a wider range of coloring possibilities. Leon Arnoux, Minton's Art Director, was responsible for naming this new ware Majolica after its fifteenth century predecessor.

Sacrifice Bowl, c. 1874-1878. "Eugenie" shaped center with light colored lead glazes. *Courtesy of the Chellis and Adams Collection.* $3,000-3,800.

Despite the great popularity of Minton's new Majolica and wide acceptance by other potters, Wedgwood did not start producing Majolica until 1860. Wedgwood believed that the company's neoclassical shapes were a mismatch to Majolica's Victorian style. Further, Wedgwood had already been producing single-color glazed wares for some time, such as their Green Glazed Ware, and did not see a need to pursue it further. However, consumer demand and lagging profits eventually forced Wedgwood to explore the growing market for Majolica.

Wedgwood's first Majolica appeared in 1860, ten years after Minton's release. Wedgwood's Majolica introduced a variety of new shapes, including sculpted figures and wares with elaborate raised designs and textures, all decorated with multi-colored glazes. Wedgwood later included shapes that were more traditional, often borrowing ideas from their stoneware pottery lines including black Basalt dolphin shaped candlesticks and Cane Ware game pie dishes. Within ten years, the number of Majolica items produced by Wedgwood exceeded all other ornamental wares they were producing at that time.

Early Wedgwood Majolica, produced from 1860-1878, utilized more vibrant colors but after 1878 the darker, more subdued colors dominated the designs. This was driven somewhat by fashion and color trends, but mainly the change was from rising health risks associated with the lead-based glazes. Brighter colored glazes meant higher concentrations of lead. Around 1900, Majolica output diminished due to pressure from the Government over lead-related health risks. Wedgwood considered healthier alternatives, but they proved too costly to produce, so Majolica production tapered off. Wedgwood terminated almost all of their Majolica production by 1910.

Types of Majolica

There are long-standing debates among collectors as to what types of wares qualify as Majolica. Wedgwood and other potters produced similar earthenware products with colored glazed as to that of Minton's Majolica. These similar wares often sold under different names according to style, theme, or fashionable buzzwords of the day making identification tedious.

Maureen Batkin offered what is frequently used as the standard for categorizing Majolica and similar glazed wares in her book, *Wedgwood Ceramics 1846-1959*. Batkin categorized the glazed wares into Monochrome, Mottled Wares, Richly Molded Ornamental Wares, Émail Ombrant Wares (French for shaded enamel), Argenta Ware, and Artistic Faience. Through examining each group, a number of similarities in production methods and composition arise, as well as the interconnectivity between the styles. Some noted authors, such as Nicholas Dawes, do consider the above-mentioned definition too broad.

Cater Jug, c. 1870. Drab colored ground. *Courtesy of the Chellis and Adams Collection.* $300-500.

Monochrome

Many collectors feel that in order for a piece to qualify as Majolica, it must contain two or more colors. The Monochromatic group utilized similar lead-glazes to Majolica, but was distinguished by the use of only one color. Wedgwood reintroduced a number of Monochromatic glazes in 1860 to compete with Majolica. Some monochromatic glazes such as Rockingham have gone on to other more elaborate uses and applications.

Rockingham Glaze

Rockingham is a glaze that uses manganese oxide as a coloring agent, to produce a purplish-brown color. A number of English potters employed this glaze for simple domestic wares as early as the 1850s, mimicking an obscure, but popular regional pottery called Rockingham Ware. Wedgwood first introduced their own Rockingham-glazed wares at the Paris Exhibition in 1878 and continued to produce them until about 1911, when the health concerns over lead-glazes ended the use of this glaze.

The name Rockingham originated from a simple brown colored Rockingham Ware that came out of the Rockingham area in Swinton, Yorkshire. Over time, Rockingham Ware became the industry name for similar brown colored wares. The glaze which came later, tended to have an almost purplish tint, giving a slightly richer look to this simple yet stylish form.

Mazarine Glaze

Mazarine Glaze is a rare blue colored version of Rockingham with essentially the same composition. It was tinted blue with the addition of cobalt. These wares were typically labeled as Rockingham. The blue was used for vases and other decorative items, adorned with Victorian-styled motifs.

Four Toby Jugs, (from left to right) Queen's Ware c. 1933, Amber glazed c. 1933, Brown glazed c. 1933, Blue glazed c. 1933. *Courtesy of the Rosen Collection.* $100-150 each.

Vigorian Ware coffee cup and saucer, c. 1878. Cauliflower, flared with "ear" handles. Deep saucer, decorated with band of buds on twigs. Cup has seven twigs with bud and blossom shaped flowers. Patterns etched by John Northwood's glass engraving firm, Perkes & Company, Stroke-On-Trent. *Courtesy of the Dorothy Lee-Jones Collection.* $300-450.

Vigornian Ware

Vigornian Ware is a form of Rockingham introduced in 1876. It had the signature Rockingham purplish-brown color on an earthenware ceramic body. What is unusual about this ware is it was decorated like glassware, using an acid-etching technique rather than enamel painting or other traditional pottery decorating methods. To accomplish this, Wedgwood employed John Northwood's glass-making firm, Perkes & Co., to acid-etch designs into the hardened Rockingham glaze. The acid would cut through the glaze and expose the underbody much in the same way glass-workers score the surface of glassware to create patterns.

Because Vigornian Ware was essentially a Rockingham colored ware, it often bore the "ROCKINGHAM" mark on the base. The decorations on Vigornian Ware typically featured a butterfly or flower motif.

Magnolia Ware

Yet another application of the Rockingham glaze is Magnolia Ware, developed by Thomas Allen of Wedgwood. The composition of Magnolia Ware could be called a stoneware because its underbody is made of Rosso Antico, Wedgwood's red-colored stoneware (see more on Rosso Antico in the Dry Bodied Stoneware chapter). We mention Magnolia Ware because it is a Rockingham derivative. In this ware colored glazes were layered and a top-most layer of Rockingham was intentionally left thin to allow a thicker pale-colored slip to show through from underneath. The purpose of this was to bring out the detailed floral motifs in a textured, almost three-dimensional effect.

Mottled Wares

Mottled Wares are a more traditional Majolica style, distinguished by random swirl or streaked multi-colored patterns. To create this effect, colored glazes were poured or splashed over the ceramic body with a brush. When fired, the colors tended to run and blend, making a natural looking flow from one color into the next. Colors used included the Rockingham brown and the Mazarine blues, greens, and yellows. This color effect was reminiscent of the old Tortoiseshell Ware from the early Wedgwood/Whieldon days of the mid-1700s.

Molded Ornamental Wares

Molded Ornamental Wares consist of multi-colored glazes, carefully hand-painted to bring out the contours and details of figures, animal shapes or heavily molded designs. Wedgwood used a number of independent artists and sculptors to produce a variety of fresh styles and shapes. These wares commonly incorporated animal shapes such as horses, dolphins or birds into their bases or stands for serving dishes, tableware and elaborate centerpieces.

Émail Ombrant Wares or Tremblay Wares

Émail Ombrant Wares (French for shaded enamel) are typically flat items such as plates or tiles, with carved or molded designs. Deep impressions were cut in the center of the piece, which were then filled with green or brown colored glaze. The excess glaze is poured off and the residue left behind pools around the edges and creates shading and a three-dimensional appearance. By varying the depths of the carved impressed design, a color contrast is achieved between light and shaded areas. These items needed to be flat to make the decorating work, since shaped objects would result in the glaze running off the piece, leading to an all-together different effect.

The Émail Ombrant style was developed in 1842 by Baron du Tremblay of France, thus is sometimes referred to as Tremblay Ware. Wedgwood acquired this process in 1873 by license and applied it to earthenware plates and dishes, marketing it as a form of Majolica. Wedgwood artists carved out shapes in the same manner as intaglio, which they then filled with translucent glaze of green, gray or blue enamel, the excess poured off and the piece re-fired to harden the glaze.

The shapes for Émail Ombrant are typically flat due to the manufacturing process, but were varied with round, octagon, as well as other shapes. To further decorate these wares, Wedgwood varied the borders with reticulations or highlights. The octagon shape is an example of a more subtle change in look. On each piece, the glazed decoration occupies the main part of the plate's center, with the outer parts decorated in simple colored enamels. The Limoge series and the Butterfly series were both distinguished by reticulated edges. The Limoge pattern incorporates straight cuts in the edges that pointed outward from the center image. The Butterfly set incorporated a lattice pattern around the outer edges, with the spaces between the lattice lines cut out. Some of the glazed decorations were simple, such as fruit or vegetable shapes. Some were more elaborate, including landscapes or scenes of people engaged in domestic activities.

Argenta Ware

Around the time of the Paris Exhibition of 1878, fashionable tastes in the pottery market began to shift away from Majolica, toward fresher, lighter wares with Japanese influences. The novelty of Majolica was also wearing off from the overflow of product by a multitude of competing potters. In addition, the health risks associated with the lead in the Majolica glazes were becoming widely known. Wedgwood responded to this shift with Argenta Ware, a Majolica derivative with a white or pale ground.

Argenta Ware was a form of Majolica with an overall lighter look, using transparent glazes on pale or white backgrounds with embossed naturalistic and oriental decoration. To distinguish this new type of Majolica, Wedgwood introduced a number of new shapes including molded animals, birds, fans, and sea creature, decorated in a Japanese-style.

Argenta Ware teapot, c. 1881-1900. Fan design. *Courtesy of the Frazier Collection.* $300-400.

The Artistic Faience

Faience is the French term for Majolica. It refers to a specific type of Majolica characterized by a plain Majolica-like glazed ceramic body, hand-painted in the style of artist Emile Lessore. Lessore's work specifically involved a Creamware body, dipped into a plain un-colored Rockingham-style glaze, upon which he hand-painted his designs.

It is hotly disputed whether Faience is truly a form of Majolica. In Harry M. Buten's book, *ABC But No Middle E*, Buten discusses that Wedgwood at one time did market Faience as Majolica. This seems to have been a marketing decision on Wedgwood's part to capitalize on the hype over Majolica wares. Since that time, Wedgwood has appropriately reclassified Lessore's work has as a form of hand-painted Creamware.

Marsden Ware

Marsden Ware is a glazed ceramic form that closely resembles Majolica, which began as a tile decoration method and then spread to other ceramic forms. George A. Marsden created these simple, textured patterns in low relief that gave the piece a hand-decorated appearance, though the tiles were mass-produced. Wedgwood procured Marsden's glazing process in 1880 by purchasing the patent directly from Marsden, who later went to work for Wedgwood.

Marsden styled tiles began production at Wedgwood in 1881. The success of Wedgwood's Marsden tiles ne-cessitated an expansion and, by 1882, Wedgwood created a separate department strictly for the production of tiles. George Marsden was hired to run the department for a brief time, which prospered until the late 1880s. Economic conditions caused a slump in the industry as a whole and in 1888 Wedgwood cut the tile department to save on costs.

In this author's opinion, Mottled Wares, Richly Molded Ornamental Wares, and Argenta Ware unquestionably qualify as Majolica. Artistic Faience however does not. As will be seen when we address that topic further on, Artistic Faience is a hand-painted form, and only uses Majolica-like glazes as a base. Majolica is all about the glaze as the glaze is the focus of attention. Monochromatic glazes have a kinship with Majolica through their composition, but do not qualify for two reasons. First, monochromatic glazes predate Minton's Majolica as introduced in 1850. They share compositional similarities, but I argue that they were brought back in 1860 during the Majolica craze, because they looked like Majolica. Marketing is a powerful business tool, but is insufficient reasoning for a reclassifying an existing class of ceramics, even for the limited purpose of advertising. Second, to determine if a ware is Majolica, I believe that it should encompass the spirit of Minton's original Majolica introduced in 1850, i.e. lead-glazed, with molded or raised designs and it should be multi-colored.

Marsden Ware Vase, c. 1885. Pinched neck, brown colored ground and textured flower design, slip decorated, 6.5". *Courtesy of the Slavid Collection.* $350-450.

Two majolica jugs, c. 1875. Celebrating the American Centennial in 1876. Both jugs feature a Washington profile (facing) and Lincoln profile (on reverse). *Courtesy of the Rosen Collection.* (Left) $550-650, (right) $500-600.

Pitcher, c. 1940. Green Glazed Ware, leaf pattern, 6.5". *Courtesy of the Frazier Collection.* $65-95.

Peace Charger, 1919. Large, 15" yellow plate of warrior with yellow armor and headpiece. Depicts *Britannia*. This is one of a three-piece set commissioned by Sloane & Smith Ltd. to commemorate the peace of 1919, (3KV mark). *Courtesy of the Rosen Collection.* $900-1,200

Plate, c. 1875. Mottled glazed pattern and raised leaf design. *Courtesy of the Horn and Hoffman Collection.* $100-150.

Plate, c. 1877. Reticulated edge and dog design from "Fresco Heads" from the Louis XV series. *Courtesy of the Slavid Collection.* $350-400.

Doric Jug, c. 1870s. Mottled Majolica, no top, with Satyr mask below the spout. WEDGWOOD mark, 7.5". *Author's Collection.* $500-600.

Plate, c. 1850. Reticulated edge with "Fresco Head" of a deer, similar to the Louis XV series, except with slightly different reticulation. *Courtesy of the Frazier Collection.* $400-500.

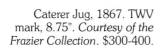

Caterer Jug, 1867. TWV mark, 8.75". *Courtesy of the Frazier Collection.* $300-400.

Plate, c. 1867-1878. Émail Ombrant style (a.k.a. Tremblay Ware), scene with girl and a wheelbarrow in center, octagon shape. *Courtesy of the Frazier Collection.* $225-275.

Dessert plate, c. 1873. Émail Ombrant style (a.k.a. Tremblay Ware), gothic scene of people and cattle. *Courtesy of the Frazier Collection.* $225-275.

Cake plate, c. 1860-1900. "Ivy Leaves on a Branch." Reticulated border, color pattern across the top resembles a sunflower motif (which was popular during the Aesthetics Movement in the 1860s-1890s). *Courtesy of the Frazier Collection.* $450-550.

Cake plate, top view. *Courtesy of the Frazier Collection.*

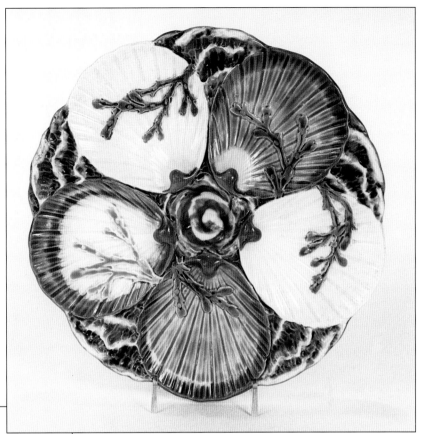

Oyster plate, c. 1870. Molded bottom (not flat) as from being pressed into a mold from behind (HNI mark), 9". *Courtesy of the Slavid Collection.* $800-1,200.

Pitcher or "Rosette Jug," c. 1865. #M1527 from the pattern book. *Courtesy of the Frazier Collection.* $350-500.

Lobster plate, c. 1870. Raised, molded relief, 8.5".
Courtesy of the Slavid Collection. $400-600.

Teapot, c. 1870. Globular form, mottled
blue, green, and brown colors, 3.5".
Courtesy of the Slavid Collection. $500-600.

Argenta Ware compote and matching dessert plate, c. 1878. Decorated with grape leaves, bushels of grapes, tendrils, strawberries, leaves, and flowers in natural colors on a white-cream ground. *Courtesy of the Dorothy Lee-Jones Collection.* Plate, $800-1,000; compote, $900-1,100.

Argenta Ware jardinière and plate, c. 1879. Both with fan design. Jardinière is 8", $400-600, plate, $200-250. *Courtesy of the Horn and Hoffman Collection.*

Argenta Ware dessert plate,
1885. Both with fan motif,
(SYN mark), 6.75". *Courtesy
of the Frazier Collection.*
$175-225.

Majolica mustard pot, c. 1875. Conical shape with
silver plate mounts by T. Harwood, turquoise
glazed interior. *Author's Collection.* $140-170.

Majolica wine ewer, c. 1875. Conical
shape with silver plate mounts by T.
Harwood and turquoise glazed interior.
Exterior in mottled greens to browns,
11.5". *Courtesy of the Dorothy Lee-
Jones Collection.* $300-400.

Marsden-style tile, c. 1881.
Designed by Lewis F. Day, 6".
*Courtesy of the Frazier
Collection.* $65-85.

Flemish Jug, c. 1870. Grey-green color,
withdrawn from production due to unaccept-
able variations in colors from firing. *Courtesy of
the Frazier Collection.* $250-280.

Chapter 4
Matte Glazed Earthenware

World War II had a strong impact on Wedgwood and the pottery industry in general, as numerous employees were called to military service. Additionally, economic conditions also cut into Wedgwood's ability to produce its decorative wares. Restrictions were put in place by the British government, limiting exportation of luxury goods. Evidently the government made one exception, allowing trade to continue with the United States. It saw this as a way to offset some of the financial aid that the United States was providing to the British for the war effort that allowed Wedgwood to produce decorative wares in limited quantities for exportation.

In this cautious economic environment, Wedgwood still managed to maintain a level of innovation and creativity as illustrated by their Matte Glazed Ware and Veronese Glazed Ware. The Matte and Veronese glazes represented a stylistic shift for Wedgwood to more contemporary looking pottery. Prior to 1929, Wedgwood's image and reputation focused on classical influences. This new approach differed greatly from their more classical styling or even their brief foray into Victorian designs seen in the latter half of the nineteenth century.

Matte Glaze — Tableware

Wedgwood first introduced Matte Glazed Ware in the 1930s. These glazes are characterized by their unique eggshell-like surface with softer more subtle colors than the Victorian-styled Majolica. Wedgwood applied these glazes over its Queen's Ware body in a number of different colors including Moonstone (white), Ravenstone (black), green, straw, blue, and grey. Matte Glazed Ware enjoyed great success due to the innovative creations of artists and designers like Keith Murray, John Skeaping, and Alan Best.

Wedgwood began producing colored matte glazes on earthenware in 1933. Unlike Majolica, this was a lead-free glaze made from a mix of China Clay, metal oxides for coloring, and a frit. The "frit" is a compound of minerals and oxides (such as Boron), which acts as a stabilizing agent in creation of the glaze. When mixed, the frit helps control the absorption of the glaze into the porous ceramic and can help reduce the toxicity of the other ingredients, making it a vast improvement of the lead-glazes of Majolica.

Large vase, 1999. Cream-colored matte finish, from the Paul Costelloe collection. *Author's Collection.* $75-110.

Matte glazes were used extensively on tableware shapes. This is where Keith Murray had his greatest input, creating a new utilitarian, Art Deco look and style to go along with the new glaze. This Art Deco look used horizontal lines and graceful curves to create a streamlined, functional appearance that embodied a futuristic-like feel. This is evident in one of the more famous matt glazed tableware patterns, Annular Ware. This was a dinnerware shape developed by Thomas Wedgwood, John Goodwin, and Keith Murray. Its most significant feature is its wide horizontal line pattern that wraps around each piece.

Artist: Keith Murray

Keith Murray was probably most responsible for the success of Wedgwood's Matte Glaze Ware in the 1930s. Murray had a simple and modernistic style that stands out among Wedgwood's more classically styled lines. Ironically, Murray did not start out working with pottery. After serving in the Royal Flying Corps during World War II, he studied to be an architect, but found work in short supply due to economic stresses of the war. In 1932, he turned to decorative glass and occasionally did some freelance design work for Wedgwood. Wedgwood hired Murray full-time in 1933 and set him to work creating innovative new shapes for Basalts, Rosso Antico, and Wedgwood's new Matte Glazes.

Murray was able to utilize his architectural training in 1936, when Josiah Wedgwood V commissioned Murray and Charles S. White to design Wedgwood's new factory in Barlaston, England.

During World War II, the British Government placed restrictions on luxury goods that could be exported abroad. Due to economic crisis and the destabilized global environment, the government allowed only basic utilitarian products to be exported. This situation led to Wedgwood's Utility Ware, introduced in 1942. Utility Ware further led to the simple yet elegant "Commonwealth" table service, a full Queen's Ware dinner set designed by Murray and introduced in 1947. This service included a series of very basic tableware shapes, designed for large-scale production and exportation.

Vase, c. 1930s. Green Matte Glazed vase with horizontal groove decoration by Keith Murray. *Courtesy of the Slavid Collection.* $700-900.

Matte Glaze – Advertising Ware

In addition to tableware, matte glazes also found use in advertising wares and for promotional items. One famous example, is the Spanish Don Decanter made for the Sandeman company. Beginning in the 1930s, the George G. Sandeman & Sons Company commissioned different potteries such as Royal Dalton, Wade, and Wedgwood to produce these collectable promotional items for marketing their liquors. The shape of the Sandeman's company logo, the Spanish Don, served as an ideal shape for advertising and promotional means. (Please note that occasionally in our modern online auctions, these bottles are referred to as "Zorro Bottles," which is a completely erroneous term.)

Royal Dalton was the first to produce a Spanish Don decanters in 1931, but as the popularity of these items grew, other potters like Wade had to be engaged to fulfill demand. Wedgwood was peripherally involved at this point, only producing molds for the decanters, but had not yet produced the decanters themselves.

In 1969, the Sandeman Company contracted with Wedgwood to produce decanters in the Spanish Don shape. The first batch consisted of 78,000 decanters, coated with Wedgwood's Ravenstone (black) Matte Glaze and contained Sandeman's Armada Cream Sherry. Half of these Spanish Don figures held a gold cup in the left hand, the other half held a gold cup in the right hand. This particular promotion coincided with the investiture of the Prince of Wales and were marked "Prince of Wales, Caernarvon, July 1969" on their base. The left-handed Spanish Don also had a feather motif marking, while the right-handed Don had a Griffin mark, both representing the Prince of Wales.

Wedgwood produced another series of Spanish Don decanters in 1970 coinciding with the Kentucky Derby. This series of Spanish Dons were glazed with Moonstone (white) Matte Glaze and contained eight-year-old scotch. The promotion celebrated the running of the racehorse Double Splash, which the Sandeman Company hoped would be the first European to win the Kentucky Derby. For this event, Wedgwood produced the same shape and design, but with slightly different markings. The first 44,420 decanters were stamped only with the Wedgwood Barlaston circle mark and the word "Moonstone." Wedgwood also produced a number of decanters with an image of a horse head and the initials "D.S." (Double Splash) followed by a number representing the potential placing of the horse in the race. There were 9,248 decanters marked with "D.S.1," 16,554 with "D.S.2," 250 with "D.S.3," and 400 with "D.S.4." The decanters were produced prior to the race, so they had different markings for the different potential outcomes. All versions were released to the public, so today's collectors are keen on acquiring one of each of the five differently marked versions.

Sandeman Spanish Don Decanter, 1977. Ravenstone glaze with ruby red cup in the right hand. Holds Partner's Port. *Author's Collection.* $30-80.

Wedgwood produced a third and final run of Sandeman Spanish Don decanters in 1977, in conjunction with the celebration of Queen Elizabeth's Royal Silver Jubilee. This was the 25th anniversary of Queen Elizabeth's coronation. These Spanish Don decanters were glazed with Ravenstone (black) and held a ruby red cup in the right hand. It is not known how many of these were made, but since they are more difficult to locate than their earlier counterparts, it can be inferred that the production may have been fewer in number.

Sculptor: John Skeaping

Matte glazes also were used in figurines and animal shapes. John Skeaping was a freelance sculptor who created a series of animal shapes for Wedgwood in 1926. Wedgwood first rendered a limited number of these animals in Black Basalt and Queen's Ware, but later mass-produced them in Matte Glazes as well. Wedgwood commissioned fourteen shapes in all, including animal shapes such as deer, polar bears, monkeys, sea lions, a tiger with a buck, kangaroos, buffalo, bison, and an antelope.

Sculptor: Alan Best

Another freelance sculptor, Alan Best, created six figures for Wedgwood in 1934-1935. Four of these were athletes rendered in Moonstone and champagne colored glazes. They included The Boxer, Olympic Weight Thrower, The Sprinter, and The Rugby Player. Alan Best also produced two animal figures, a Mandarin duck figure rendered in a celadon and ivory colored Matte Glaze as well as a panther shape rendered in cream and brown colored glaze.

Veronese Glazed Ware

Between the American stock market crash in 1929 and World War II, orders for decorative Jasper Ware all but stopped in the 1930s. In 1933 Norman Wilson, Wedgwood's Production Director, introduced Veronese Glazed Ware as a way to keep his highly skilled pottery throwers employed. Veronese Glazed Ware is strikingly similar to Matte Glaze Ware, but was used more for decorative items than tableware. It had a more satin-like finish with colors that included red, purple, blue, turquoise, green, yellow, and black. It also appeared in two different forms: one with luster highlighting and a version with plain stain glaze that is sometimes mistaken for matte glaze.

Polar Bear figure, c. 1935-1939. Straw matt glaze, mounted on wood base. By John Skeaping. *Courtesy of the Slavid Collection.* $600-700.

Veronese Glazed Ware combined simple, inexpensive glazes with fancier shapes that justified keeping the skilled potters employed. This effectively reduced the average costs relative to the more costly Jasper production. The less expensive Veronese continued to sell while the more expensive wares languished. Veronese Wares continued in production until about 1941 when World War II was in full swing. Due to problems with government regulation and the economic downturn, almost all decorative wares began dropping off in favor of Utility Wares.

Artist: Erling (Eric) B. Olsen

Eric Olsen served as a freelance artist with Wedgwood from 1931-1935. Olsen sculpted a number of Art Deco shapes, which Wedgwood would decorate with their Matte and Veronese glazes. His work resembled that of Keith Murray's modernistic designs though Olsen incorporated subtle Grecian themes into his decorations. Murray also focused his shapes on a wide range of ornamental pieces; Olsen focused more on everyday items such as cigarette boxes, ashtrays, bookends, inkwells, and lamps.

Designer: Norman Wilson

Norman Wilson began his ceramics career by running his family's china business when his father became ill. While working he continued his education, after which Wedgwood offered him a Works Manager position at the Etruria factory in 1927. There he helped develop a number of new ceramic shapes and worked with Matte Glazed Ware until he was called to serve in World War II. Upon Norman Wilson's return from service in 1946, Wedgwood appointed him Production Director at the Barlaston factory. He later retired in 1963.

Unique Wares

In addition to Norman Wilson's administrative and operational work for Wedgwood, he also produced Unique Wares, a limited collection of radically new contemporary and art deco-styled wares. The first Unique Wares were produced by Wedgwood between 1932-1939 and some additional Unique Wares were produced from 1954-1963. These uniquely styled pieces were considered outside the mainstream Wedgwood items.

Wilson concentrated on more creative means of decorating wares than on the shapes themselves — taking pre-made shapes and applying his own designs to them. Some of these unusual designs may appear to resemble Majolica, but the glazes are of different composition and have an altogether different styling than the ninetieth century Majolica glazes. One technique that Wilson employed was the layering on of different colored glazes. This often had the result of a subtle blend of color showing through the top-most layer. It also allowed Wilson to experiment with "sgraffito," a method of incising design patterns into the ceramic body, cutting through the outer layer of colored slip to the ceramic body underneath. The color contrast between the slip and ceramic body brought out patterns and textures, which were then glazed. Harry Barnard also used this decorative technique as well (additional information is available on Barnard in the Jasper section). Most of Wilson's work was marked with his initials, "NW," in addition to other typical Wedgwood markings.

Lidded powder bowl, c. 1930-1940. Speckled rust glaze. By Norman Wilson. *Courtesy of the Slavid Collection.* $700-900.

Twentieth Century Glazes: Michael Dillion & Paul Costelloe

Michael Dillon (1944-1976) was an art student at Bendingo Technical College in Victoria, Canada, before moving to England. He joined Wedgwood in 1970 and was allowed to pursue his own sculpting style, creating Oriental-inspired shapes, abstract clay designs, and special glazes. The originality in his work sets Dillion apart from the more traditional styles Wedgwood is known for. Dillon's trademark on most of his pieces is characterized by a pinched top. Unfortunately, Dillion was killed in an accident in 1976, tragically cutting short a promising artistic career.

In 1999, Wedgwood revived matte glazes to produce a special line of wares designed by famous fashion designer, Paul Costelloe. Wedgwood describes the line as "contemporary earthenware" with simple, yet elegant shapes decorated with soft matte glazes of cream, grey, and limestone. These wares are dated and should have Costelloe's symbol of a running fox printed somewhere unobtrusively on each piece.

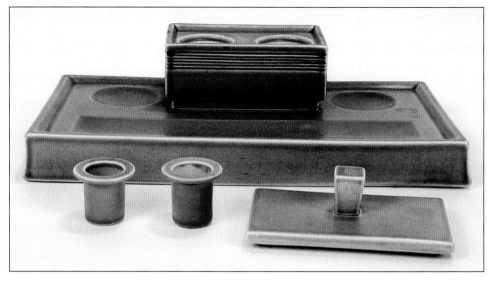

Ink stand, disassembled view.

Ink stand, c. 1933-1938. Green Matte Glazed, two removable ink pots in rectangular holder with cover, designed by Keith Murray, *Courtesy of the Dorothy Lee-Jones Collection.* $500-700.

Tankard, c. 1930. Green Matte Glazed, by Keith Murray. *Author's Collection.* $150-180.

Bookends, c. 1932. Green Veronese Glazed, "Pan" design by Erling (Eric) Olsen, 6.5". *Courtesy of the Slavid Collection.* $1,200.

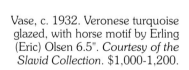

Vase, c. 1932. Veronese turquoise glazed, with horse motif by Erling (Eric) Olsen 6.5". *Courtesy of the Slavid Collection.* $1,000-1,200.

Two Monkeys, c. 1939. On rectangular base, matte-champagne colored, by John Skeaping, 6 7/8" x 3". *Courtesy of the Dorothy Lee-Jones Collection.* $700-800.

Leopard figure, c. 1945. Designed by Arnold Machin. Brownish-red (terracotta-like) clay, coated with Norman Wilson created gray and brown glazes, 6.25". *Courtesy of the Slavid Collection.* $1,000.

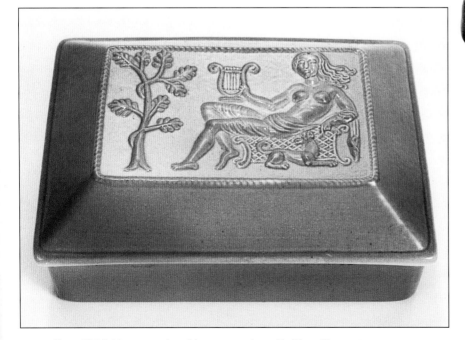

Box, 1946. Veronese glazed box, turquoise with *Muse Erato at her lyre* design by Arnold Machin (6B46 mark, Wedgwood circular stamp). *Courtesy of the Slavid Collection.* $500-600.

Vase, c. 1940s. Cylindrical, dripped brown glaze, textured, 9.5", by Norman Wilson. *Courtesy of the Slavid Collection*. $1,000.

Pilgrim Flask, c. 1940s. Green Matte Glazed flask by Norman Wilson. *Courtesy of the Slavid Collection*. $800-1,200.

Stoneware vase, c. 1970. In the shape of an African Hut, with decorative streaked matt brown glaze, designed by Michael Dillon, signed by Dillon. *Courtesy of the Frazier Collection*. $600-700.

Shell shaped plate, c. 1957. Moonstone glaze, 11". *Author's Collection*. $60-75.

Vase, 1964. Ravenstone glaze, 6.5" (10 B 64 mark). *Courtesy of the Frazier Collection*. $55-75.

Candle holder, 1999. Matt grey glaze, by famous fashion designer Paul Costelloe. *Courtesy of the Frazier Collection.* $20-40.

Vinegar bottle, 1999. White matte glaze design by fashion designer Paul Costelloe. Features Costelloe's signature and his symbol, the silhouette of a running fox. 11". This piece is usually paired with a grey oil bottle of the same shape and size. *Courtesy of the Frazier Collection.* $50-100.

Chapter 5

Black Basalt

During the mid-1700s, a popular stoneware was produced in England called Egyptian Black. It had an unglazed, matte-black finish and was produced in a variety of shapes that were generally simple in design such as tea sets and other useful items. Egyptian Black wares, made from red clays that turned black when fired, had been around for centuries; however, the Egyptian Black of the mid-1700s utilized a different type of clay and was stained with "car" to achieve its black color. Car is an oxide that naturally occurs as a byproduct of coal and was found in sediment from drainage out of local coal deposits. At this time, coal was used heavily to heat the kilns in English potteries.

Egyptian Black was a common product in Staffordshire, as local clays and colorings were plentiful. The Black, as it was also referred to, represented a growing trend in pottery, fueled by a handful of famous explorers and their stories of adventures to Egypt and other foreign lands. Egyptian styled art and pottery were quickly becoming the symbol of sophistication and fashion in England. The name Egyptian Black, referred to its resemblance to black Egyptian statues, vases, and other works of art that were being brought back from Egypt. These were often made of matte-finished black marble, distinctive of Egyptian artifacts.

In the 1760s, Wedgwood was looking for a new medium to explore additional avenues of creative ceramic expression. Wedgwood saw Egyptian Black as offering enormous untapped potential, but the clay mixtures of the day were flawed and the pieces imperfect. Like other stonewares of the time, Black consisted of heavy clay, which was thick, bulky, and unable to handle fine or complicated artistic applications. Stoneware had its own niche in the home ceramics market, but was considered lesser in quality than its delicate and stylish earthenware counterpart. Though consumers sought these Egyptian Black wares, Wedgwood knew something had to be done to make them a viable long-term product that could compete in the same markets as porcelain and cream-colored earthenware.

Wedgwood began his experimentation with Black in 1767, spending a number of years refining and perfecting his formulas. He showed the same fervor for experimentation and commitment to perfection that he had in development of his Creamware. Wedgwood encoun-

tered a variety of problems with his first experiments, such as how to lighten the ceramic body without making it brittle. Numerous experimental pieces were lost due to breakage, prompting many formula revisions. Eventually he succeeded and in 1768 introduced his Black Porcelain, a.k.a. Black Etruscan, which he later renamed Black Basalt.

Bust of Homer, c. 1790, 11.5". *Courtesy of the Chellis and Adams Collection.* $700-900.

Black Basalt was named for its similarity to the naturally occurring Basalt rocks that lined the English seashore. This new improved Black Basalt had little resemblance to the older Black. It almost rivaled Wedgwood's Creamware with its range of shapes and uses. Black Basalt rapidly gained popularity due to its remarkably smooth texture and a richer, more vibrant black color than its predecessors. This resulted from chemical composition improvements that Wedgwood made. For instance, the older Egyptian Black primarily consisted of local Bradwell clay mixed with ochre, a coloring oxide. Wedgwood's Black Basalt did not use the local clay, but rather a mix of black iron oxide, manganese oxide, and Purbeck clay. This resulted in a darker and richer black color. In addition, each piece was lightweight and yet had a strength and durability never before seen in Egyptian Black wares. The dynamic shapes and revolutionary quality helped Black Basalt surpass the older Egyptian Black and achieve a dominant position in the black stoneware market.

Basalt worked well in both useful and artistic applications which allowed Wedgwood to venture into new areas of decoration and designs not seen in their other ceramics. With Wedgwood's Creamware poised to take over the lead in the tableware and common goods markets, Wedgwood focused his Black Basalt on shapes and designs that would compliment his other works.

Though Black Basalt would end up being produced in a variety of unusual shapes, the first Basalt items to come from Wedgwood included unpainted vases, cameos, busts, and intaglios. Since Basalt resisted acids and could withstand heat, it was soon applied to tableware and tea wares. The tea sets were an interesting and unintended success. Black tea wares had been quite popular during the eighteenth century because of a fashion obsession with fair skin. The women of the time went to great efforts to maintain white skin and they enjoyed the black wares since they would offer a flattering contrast to their fair-skinned hands. Other useful items also emerged such as flower bulb pots, oil lamps, chocolate pots, and inkwells, but of all the shapes Wedgwood produced, the ones that commanded the most interest were the Basalt vases.

Basalt Designs and Quality

Josiah Wedgwood had a particular affinity for vases of a classical nature. Vases at this time had become fashionable status symbols by the affluent members of high society. Wedgwood's early Basalt designs quickly distinguished themselves with a more traditional approach than those of his neoclassical predecessors by drawing upon established antique styles of Greek, Roman, Egyptian, and even Italian influences. This was a break from the traditional mainstay of Staffordshire potteries. In fact, a number of Wedgwood's shapes were reproductions of classical antique vases in the collections of his more wealthy supporters. Wedgwood was the first, and for a time, the only potter to undertake this new classical approach. He went on to create a trend toward these classically styled, antique vases.

Many have said that Wedgwood was a perfectionist, as he had a tremendous focus on the quality of vases that his potters produced. Wedgwood personally supervised the production lines and was known to occasionally smash and destroy items that he felt were not up to the Wedgwood standard of perfection. These stories support the common belief that the Wedgwood factory produced no "seconds" (imperfect items), but this is not completely true. Wedgwood despised flaws created by human hands, but damages created during firing occasionally would be fixed or altered, as Wedgwood stated, "It was the will of the fire which man cannot fully control."

Decorations on Basalt were not always artistically driven. Often decorations were used to fix or disguise firing damage to make a damaged piece sellable. Silver was sometimes applied to the rims or edges of items in part to decorate, but also to cover chips or other imperfections. Bronzed Encaustic was a form of Basalt that evolved out of a need to cover up imperfections. During Wedgwood's experiments with Basalt, it would have been too costly to discard every piece in which he found a flaw, so he bronzed a number of items in order to smooth out or conceal imperfections. This was not a radical move, in that the Basalt of the early period had a slight glossy sheen to it that made it look akin to antique bronze. This slight glossy sheen was another difference between Basalt and the traditional Egyptian Black wares that came before it. Wedgwood also took Bronzed Encaustic a step further, using gold powder to create a simulated bronze coating. While these items were well received, they were not purposely created in any great quantity. Wedgwood was so proud of his Basalt that he called it "Sterling" and noted, "It will last forever."

Thomas Bentley

One of the most influential business relationships in Wedgwood's history was that of Josiah Wedgwood's partnership with Thomas Bentley. The partnership was sealed in November of 1768, and in 1769, when Wedgwood opened his new Etruria factory, Bentley took over running it while Wedgwood spent most of his time in the Burslem factory. Though few pieces were attributed specifically to Bentley, it was Bentley's job to oversee and direct the production of fine ornamental wares at the Etruria factory. By the time the opening of Etruria occurred, the popularity of Basalt had grown so much so that supply could not keep up with demand. Wedgwood directed Bentley to focus all the new factory's efforts on turning out Basalt ornamental wares.

Bentley also served a valuable role behind the scenes at Wedgwood. He and Wedgwood corresponded daily via hand-written letters discussing experimental works, new shapes, clays, how the public was receiving their wares, as well as the latest trends. They collaborated on a number of new designs and Wedgwood would often consult Bentley who would suggest improvements. Basalt vases of the Wedgwood/Bentley period are typically identified by "Wedgwood & Bentley" marks. These pieces are prized possessions of modern-day collectors.

Encaustic Painted Decoration

One of the more famous forms of decoration that Wedgwood utilized on Basalt pieces was Encaustic Painting. This was a hand-painting method that Wedgwood perfected and patented in 1769. Wedgwood developed Encaustic Painting in imitation of Greek and Roman styles. Wedgwood favored a style of red or white paint on matte-finished Basalt that could be hand painted thinly and precisely. Images from old Greek pottery were glossy and had a great deal less definition, whereas Wedgwood's patterns were sharp and detailed. In addition, Wedgwood's pieces had a subtle, classical look that both honored the antiques they were meant to imitate and introduced something new to the style.

One of the more famous Encaustic Painted vase designs was the First Day Vase, produced on June 13, 1769, marking the opening of Wedgwood's new factory at Etruria. The shape, number 302, from the Wedgwood pattern books, mimicked a classical Greek shape. Text was added to the decoration utilizing encaustic painting, announcing the new factory and date.

Enameled Decoration

Enameled decoration was widely used on Basalt and took several different forms. Beginning in 1810, Wedgwood applied enameled decoration in the Famille Rose style as a revival of an old Chinese technique of opaque enameling in shades of pink, rose, and purple.

Teapot and cover, c. 1769-1780. Bamboo Ware-styled body, (Impressed mark: "Wedgwood & Bentley"). *Courtesy of the Frazier Collection.* $5,000-6,000.

Capri Ware was a similar decoration to the Famille Rose, introduced in 1860. These designs incorporated hand-painted Chinese floral patterns. The Capri is generally considered a lesser quality version of the Famille style since the Famille enameling is a raised form of layers of hand-applied paint and detailing. The Capri is very flat and simpler in detail.

Flat candlestick, c. 1820. Encaustic painted decoration. *Courtesy of the Slavid Collection.* $800.

Kenlock Ware

Kenlock Ware was a form of enamel decorated Black Basalt or Rosso Antico made in limited quantities by Wedgwood from 1895 to 1900. Kennard Wedgwood, founder of the North American subsidiary of Wedgwood, developed this form using established enamel painting techniques. What made these different from other enameled wares were the design and patterns developed by Kennard Wedgwood in two primary variations, dragon and iris. As their names suggest, the dragon Kenlock wares were decorated with Chinese dragon designs and the iris with hand-painted iris flowers. These wares are usually easy to identify as their bases printed with the mark "Dragon Kenlock Ware" or "Iris Kenlock Ware" along with the other Wedgwood markings.

A rare and hard to find form of Kenlock Ware is the Golf Girl series. There were several designs of these female golf scenes, applied to different shapes, notably the Cambridge Ale jug shape. These were designed by freelance artist Christopher Dresser, who created a number of other designs for tableware and ornamental pieces between 1865-1880 for Wedgwood.

Auro Basalt

Auro Basalt is a very unusual branch of Basalt and is similar to Golconda Ware in its designs and technique (refer to Bone China, Chapter 8). Auro Basalt is distinguished by raised gold relief, which is thinner and less defined than a Jasper relief, applied to the Basalt body. The overall design imitates Japanese Bronze, with gilded and bronzed raised-slip forming leaves and floral patterns. The Auro Basalt was produced in limited supply around 1885.

Engine Turning Decoration

Engine turning was a style of lathe carving on Basalt that cut patterns into the surface of the pottery. The pottery piece was placed on its side and spun in a horizontal direction while the potter touched the piece with a cutting tool. The motion of the spinning piece against the cutting tool would create a uniform indentation. The engine turned lathe was an invention that was in use prior to Wedgwood's time, but Wedgwood was able to improve it so the lathe could turn a piece upright to allow flutes, zigzags, checkers, and chevrons to be engraved into the surface. This led to the popular Dice Ware style in Wedgwood's Jasper ceramic.

Black Basalt vs. Black Jasper

Confusion often arises, especially in on-line auctions and flea markets, in trying to identify Black Basalt versus Black Jasper. Older pieces of Basalt are easier to identify since older Basalt often has a polished sheen to its surface, whereas Black Jasper always has a matte surface. Modern-day Basalt however has a texture closer in finish to Jasper, due in part to the use of molds and the methods of mass-production. In the past, texture could also reveal clues to production dates, but these modern day mass production methods have made the texture much more similar.

Another way to distinguishing between the two ceramics is the application of white relief. Wedgwood does not use white relief on Black Basalt due to chemical composition incompatibilities. This incompatibility focuses mainly around their shrinkage rates during firing. The two ceramics shrink at different rates in the kilns, causing the applied relief to pop off the surface. Black Jasper, conversely, is commonly found with some form of white Jasper ornamentation. In the past century, Basalt has had different forms of applied decoration such as gold gilding, which nicely complemented the look and feel of the Basalt. Unlike the Black Jasper, Basalt is a touchstone for gold and to find the two together is common. Various forms of Encaustic Painting were also widely used for decoration, yet rarely ever seen on Jasper. Rosso Antico has also appeared on Basalt and Ba salt ornamentation has appeared as decoration on Rosso Antico. Glazing of table and serving wares is more prevalent on Basalt, as opposed to Jasper, which was used for more decorative wares (see Jasper Ware, Chapter 6).

Artist: Ernest William Light

An artist who stands out with his work with Black Basalt at Wedgwood is a sculptor by the name of Ernest William Light. Light was an artist, a modeler, and an art teacher who was commissioned by Wedgwood in 1913 to sculpt a series of animal figures in Basalt. Bird figures were his main focus in this series, including Alighting Bird, Cockatoo, Crane Egret, Flamingo, Kingfisher, Pelican, Raven Toy Jap Bird, Woodpecker, and four versions of birds in flight. He also produced figures of a bear, bulldog, cat, butterfly, elephant, poodle, rabbit, and squirrel. Light went to work for Royal Dalton in 1914, so no further Wedgwood items were done by Light beyond that point.

Copies of these original Light figures were reissued in 1935. The difference between the two can be found in the eyes. In the earlier version, the figures have glass eyes, when the reissue took place in 1935 the eyes were made of the same Basalt clay as the figures themselves.

Raven figure, c. 1913. Features glass eyes, designed by Ernest Light. *Courtesy of the Chellis and Adams Collection.* $400-600.

Artist: George Stubbs

George Stubbs was a famous painter who specialized in animal forms, particularly in horses. He is credited with the first accurate and detailed drawing of horse anatomy. Stubbs studied the horse form in every detail, including the first detailed dissection and cataloging of the horse body and components.

Stubbs contacted Wedgwood looking for large Queen's Ware plaques upon which to try his hand at enamel painting. Stubbs painted a number of these without any great commercial success at the time. At the time

his death, the recovered ceramic works were not viewed as saleable quality, but today are considered near priceless. A selection of painted Queen's Ware plaques are on display at the Lady Lever Art Gallery in Port Sunlight, Liverpool, UK. The two most famous Wedgwood works attributable to Stubbs were two Basalt plaques depicting the Frightened Horse modeled in 1780 and the Fall of Phaeton. These forms were later used to create Basalt and Jasper plaques under the same names.

Basalt medallion of Josiah Wedgwood, c. 1790, $500-700. Oval medallion inlayed text in white, c. 1784. "FRS" (Fellow of Royal Society) No. 133, awarded to Josiah Wedgwood for his invention of the pyrometer, was given out in case with pyrometer when sold. $600-800. *Both courtesy of the Horn and Hoffman Collection.*

Teapot, c. 1790. Fluted shape with widow finial, (WEDGWOOD mark). *Courtesy of the Chellis and Adams Collection.* $500-800.

Two busts. (Left) Robert Burns, 8", modeled by E. W. Wyon, c. 1870, $900-950. (Right) Newton, rare, (Wedgwood & Bentley mark), c. 1775, $1,100-1,300. *Courtesy of the Horn and Hoffman Collection.*

Cup & Saucer, c. 1780-1790. Black Basalt with iron red encaustic painted anthemion style decoration. *Courtesy of the Chellis and Adams Collection.* $600-700.

113

Fern pot, c. 1790s. Scalloped edge, lattice work, and floral designs. Interior has impressions from hand-pressing the piece into a mold. *Author's Collection*. $650-750.

Cider mug, c. 1780. Black Basalt with silver rim, (WEDGWOOD & BENTLEY mark). *Courtesy of the Chellis and Adams Collection.* $1,000-1,200.

Two portrait medallions, c. 1779. Depicting Lord Charles Pratt Camden after a medal by Thomas Pingo, both marked: Wedgwood & Bentley. (Left) Basalt, with a scooped back for firing, 2.5" x 3.5", $700-900. (Right) Jasper with two firing holes in the back for firing, 1.5" x 1.25", $400-600. *Courtesy of the Horn and Hoffman Collection.*

Creamer, c. 1800s. Black Basalt in Arabian style. *Courtesy of the Chellis and Adams Collection.* $250-350.

Satyr mugs (pair) with handles, c. 1800s. (Wedgwood mark.) *Courtesy of the Chellis and Adams Collection.* Pair: $500-550.

Inkwell, c. late-1700s. Black Basalt with encaustic painted borders. Mark: "WEDGWOOD." *Courtesy of the Chellis and Adams Collection.* $300-400.

Oval plaque, c. late-1700s to early-1800s. Depicts *Judgment of Hercules*, (has a "J" potter's mark), 11.5". *Courtesy of the Chellis and Adams Collection.* $800-900.

Candlestick, c. late-1700s. Black Basalt with Egyptian motifs. Mark: "WEDGWOOD." *Courtesy of the Chellis and Adams Collection.* $300-400.

Covered sugar pot, c. early 1800s. Black Basalt with enameled Famille Rose styled decorations. Mark: "WEDGWOOD." *Courtesy of the Chellis and Adams Collection.* $400-650.

Coffee pot, c. early 1800s. Black Basalt with enameled Famille Rose styled decorations, mark: "WEDGWOOD." *Courtesy of the Chellis and Adams Collection.* $450-750.

Spill Vase, c. 1800. Muse designs, 4.75". *Courtesy of the Frazier Collection.* $200-300.

Enameled covered pot, c. early 1800s. Black Basalt. Potter's mark only, 5" high, Famille Rose styled decoration. *Courtesy of the Chellis and Adams Collection.* $350-400.

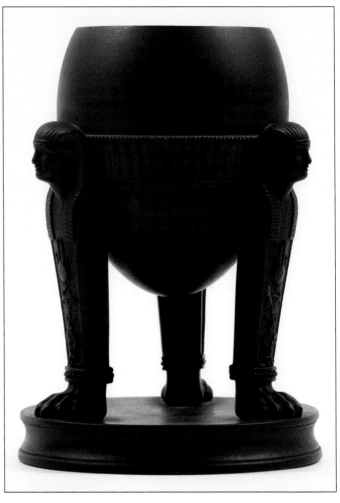

Pastille burner (cover missing), 1805. Black Basalt with Egyptian Sphinx motifs. Mark: large impressed "WEDGWOOD," bottom print reads, "Josiah Wedgwood Feb. 1805," 6 5/8". *Courtesy of the Chellis and Adams Collection.* $180-200.

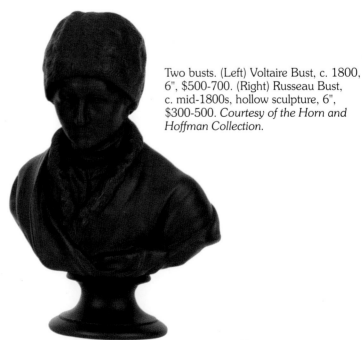

Two busts. (Left) Voltaire Bust, c. 1800, 6", $500-700. (Right) Russeau Bust, c. mid-1800s, hollow sculpture, 6", $300-500. *Courtesy of the Horn and Hoffman Collection.*

Teapot, c. early 1800s. Cabbage shape in Black Basalt. *Courtesy of the Chellis and Adams Collection.* $400-600.

Powder shaker, c. late 1700s. Black Basalt with sterling silver top with holes in for dispensing powder, mark: "WEDGWOOD." *Courtesy of the Chellis and Adams Collection.* $275-325.

Viol Del Gamba vase, c. 1801-1803, 6.5". *Courtesy of the Slavid Collection.* $500-550.

Two medallions, c. 1815. Both depict General Blucher, Prince of Wahlstadt and Field Marshall of Prussia. (Left) white smear-glazed stoneware, $200-300, (right) is Basalt, $300-400. *Courtesy of the Horn and Hoffman Collection.*

Pair of Basalt medallions Napoleon (Italios), c. 1805. *Battle of Maringo* and *Baptism of the King of Rome*, 2.5". *Courtesy of the Horn and Hoffman Collection.* $500-700 each.

Vase, c. 1810-1820. Portland shape with enameled Famille Rose decoration, Chinese flowers. This style was called Capri Ware in later produced versions, but they lack the quality of their earlier counterparts, (moustache marks), authenticated. *Courtesy of the Frazier Collection.* $375-475.

Intaglio, c. 1800. Depicts Thomas Jefferson, front reads,
"My Country" (Wedgwood mark), 1" x .75". *Courtesy of
the Horn and Hoffman Collection.* $200-300.

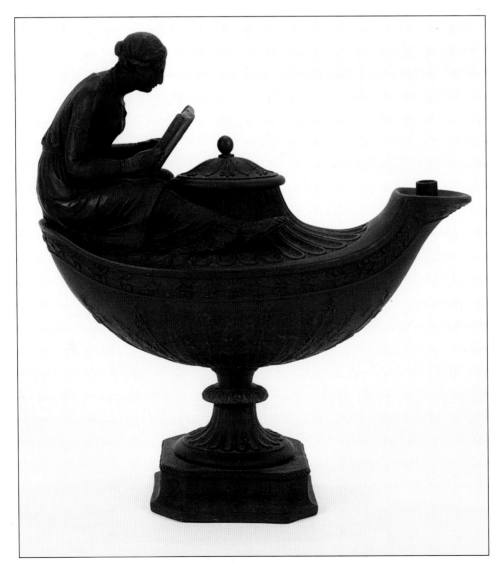

Reading (oil) lamp, c.
1820s. Removable lid/
top, companion to the
Vestle Lamp, 9" x 9.5".
*Courtesy of the Chellis
and Adams Collection.*
$1,300-1,500.

Pastille burner, c. 1820. Tripod design, Egyptian styled, with removable serrated top. Each of the three legs consists of a female body with Egyptian headdress and lion paw at the base. 10". *Courtesy of the Slavid Collection.* $1,750.

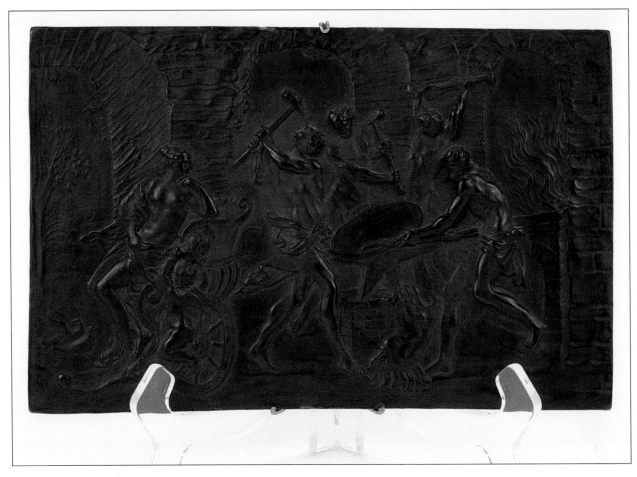

Tablet, c. 1800s. Scene is *Vulcan at the Forge watched by Venus in Her Chariot*, 10". *Courtesy of the Chellis and Adams Collection.* $700-900.

Tablet, c. 1830. Depicts the *Death of a Roman Warrior* a.k.a. *Death of Meleager*, 18 7/8" x 10". *Courtesy of the Horn and Hoffman Collection.* $4,000-5,000.

Medallion, c. mid-1800s. Mounted relief depicting *Hercules and the Nemean Lion*, (Wedgwood mark), 6" x 8". *Courtesy of the Horn and Hoffman Collection.* $500-600.

Bust of Lord Byron, c. 1860s. Sculpted by Wyon, 15". *Courtesy of the Horn and Hoffman Collection.* $600-800.

Nubian water carrier, c. 1880. Native girl figure wearing grass skirt and standing next to a piece of pottery. *Courtesy of the Slavid Collection.* $900.

Large Pitcher, c. 1900. Black Basalt, Dragon Kenlock Ware with enameled Chinese Dragon designs and rope handle, "Dragon Kenlock Ware" printed on bottom. *Courtesy of the Chellis and Adams Collection.* $600-700.

Cambridge Ale shaped Jug, c. 1900. Kenlock Ware with *Lady Golfer* enameled design, originally drawn by Christopher Dresser. *Courtesy of the Slavid Collection.* 1,000.

Bulldog figure, c. 1913. Brown glass eyes, by Ernest William Light, 3" x 5". *Courtesy of the Dorothy Lee-Jones Collection*. $600-800.

Tumbler, c. 1919. Foliate beadwork around the sides, carved "WWB 1/9/19" on the bottom, 3.25". These tumblers were for visitors to the Etruria Factory. The visitors were allowed to take part in their manufacture and sign the bottoms. The factory would then fire the piece and mail it to the visitor's home. *Courtesy of the Slavid Collection*. $200-300.

Squirrel figure, c. 1913. Glass eyes, by Ernest William Light. *Courtesy of the Chellis and Adams Collection*. $400-600.

Two medallions produced from the same mold, depicting author Jonathan Swift. Basalt medallion (Wedgwood & Bentley mark), c. pre-1780. White on blue Jasper medallion (Burt Bentley mark), c. 1920. *Courtesy of the Horn and Hoffman Collection.* $300-500 each.

Medallion, c. 1920. From a guild seal made for Arthur Cook, (Wedgwood, O marks). *Courtesy of the Horn and Hoffman Collection.* $200-300.

Medallion, 1922. Rosso Antico relief of *Baroness de Rothschild* made by Burt Bentley, probably as a trial piece (Wedgwood, O marks, incised: "21/4/22 stained orange with red figure"). *Courtesy of the Horn and Hoffman Collection.* $350-450.

Portrait Medallion, c. 1970. Depicts Beethoven, front reads, "1770 to 1827." *Courtesy of the Frazier Collection.* $120-150.

Seal figure, c. 1927. Designed by J. Skeaping. *Courtesy of the Slavid Collection.* $800-1,000.

Mini coffee can, mini cup and saucer, c. 1990s. *Author's Collection.* Each: $25-30.

Mercury Figure, 1975. 11.25". *Courtesy of the Frazier Collection*. $270-300.

Plaque, 1976. Gold gilding of a scene depicting *Lord of the Diadems* from a limited edition of 3,000. *Author's Collection*. $180-200.

Slave Medallion, c. 1970s. Black Basalt, reproduction commissioned by the Wedgwood Collector's Society. Mark: "WEDGWOOD," "MADE IN ENGLAND," printed "Wedgwood Collector's Society." *Courtesy of the Chellis and Adams Collection*. $75-95.

Chapter 6
Jasper Ware

Josiah Wedgwood had numerous innovations to his credit in the field of ceramics, but the one truly remarkable and entirely original invention was his Jasper Ware. Jasper is a dry-bodied stoneware, which means it had an unglazed, matte-finished surface that was very suitable for applied relief. Jasper was the result of over 10,000 recorded experiments by Wedgwood and represented the most significant advancement in ceramics since the Chinese invention of porcelain centuries earlier. Jasper also had the distinction of being the first ceramic created specifically for ornamental ware.

When many hear the name Wedgwood, an image invariably comes to mind of blue and white Jasper. Its smooth texture, classically decorative designs, and color scheme make it one of the most popular and well-known collectable ceramics. Many have tried to copy it and adopt its name for their own wares, but today Jasper is synonymous with the name Wedgwood.

Development

The innovation of Jasper was motivated in large part by a rapidly growing interest in antique Grecian gems. These gems were originally made from stone and shell, but in the 1770s glass cameo reproductions, which took a great deal of time, effort, and money to produce, were gaining popularity in England.

Around this time, Wedgwood's business was gaining momentum with his Queen's Ware and Black Basalt. Wedgwood recognized the growing trend in cameos, and wondered if a ceramic cameo might be easier and less expensive to produce. Since there were no existing ceramic bodies that exhibited similar characteristics to that of a glass cameo, he realized he would need to create one. Wedgwood knew the difficult task would be creating something that would have a level of quality synonymous with the Wedgwood name and that could compete directly with the glass manufacturers.

Wedgwood's idea for a new ceramic was one that would be perfectly white after firing, allowing it to be tinted in a range of desirable colors simulating natural cameos. In addition, the body had to be a hard, vitreous surface to endure polishing. Vitrification is the process of firing the clay at a high heat to turn the clay into a non-porous, almost glass-like substance, which protects the surface

without glazing. The surface also had to be hard enough to withstand lapidary polishing, which was used on tea wares intended to hold hot liquids as well as prevent staining and discoloration during everyday use. The lapidary process was also used to polish the edges of cameos for the Greek gem look. Many years later, Wedgwood discontinued this polishing step on their cameos and today's versions are made with a simple matte-finish.

Covered Vase, c. 1980. Black-dip with white stripes and relief depicting *Dancing Hours* figures. From the "Masterpiece Series" collection. *Courtesy of the Frazier Collection.* $700-800.

Creating a perfectly white clay body was the first obstacle Wedgwood had to address. Most ceramic clays had impurities, such as traces of iron, which would cause a brown tint in the finished product. Wedgwood's early experiments resulted in a color closer to yellow or light brown, rather than white. He experimented with a number of clays such as Cornish and even some imported Cherokee and Chinese clay. The other side of the equation, and equally important, was the need for a fusible stone in the mix. When fired, fusible stone is the key element in making the vitrification process work. Though fusible stone sources were available in nearby Cornwall, most were unpredictable when mixed with other ceramic ingredients. Some experiments melted to a glass-like state and others simply were not hard enough.

Though Wedgwood began experimentation in 1771, his prospering business kept him busy and lengthened the experiment period on his new ceramic. It took years to strike the right balance of ingredients that would fulfill his needs for color and quality, as well as be cost effective, and reliable for mass-production. In 1774, Wedgwood discovered a mixture that would work, giving him the necessary result each time. This mixture was finally able to produce a ceramic body free of imperfection that could be easily tinted to a desired range of colors and could be polished on a lapidary wheel for a fine finish.

Portrait medallion, c. 1775. White on blue depicting *Aristophanes* (Wedgwood and Bentley mark). *Courtesy of the Horn and Hoffman Collection.* $500-600.

Another innovation that Wedgwood introduced through his Jasper experiments was a relief made separately from the ceramic body to achieve a cameo effect. The relief was applied to a cheese hard, unfired body, and then the entire piece was fired. Before this time, the only way to achieve contrasting colors on raised images was through hand painting, but even this produced poor quality. Wedgwood explained his idea to Bentley in a letter dated December 18, 1774: "*I propose making the heads of this composition, and sometimes the grounds, but each separate. The grounds must be cut even and polished, and the underside of the heads ground even so as to lie perfectly flatt [sic] upon the polished ground.*" Josiah was describing the method known as sprigging in which the relief is made separately from the body and applied to the body's surface before firing. The result was a delicate and altogether more skillful method of decoration than any surface-painting method.

By 1775, Wedgwood's new ceramic was ready and the name Jasper began appearing in advertising to describe his "fine white composition." These early Jasper pieces were mainly small items such as the cameos, seals, and small portraits. Larger items had not been attempted yet as adjustments were needed to ensure proper firing. Wedgwood continued refining and perfecting his Jasper, producing his best works after 1780. Though Wedgwood consulted and collaborated with Thomas Bentley on Jasper's development, Bentley never saw Jasper at its peak. Bentley died in 1780, and though Wedgwood and Bentley are well known for their vases as well as other creations in Basalt, no Jasper vase has ever sported a "Wedgwood & Bentley" mark.

James Tassie was a Scottish sculptor and artist, whose name frequently arises from this period. Tassie became one of the foremost glass-workers in England and he was both a competitor of Wedgwood as well as a friend and collaborator. At the time Wedgwood was producing his ceramic solution to the gem cameo, Tassie was producing his glass cameo versions. Tassie was well known for his medallions, seals, and cameos utilizing a glass-like paste of his own creations. Tassie also made cameo molds for Wedgwood.

Solid Jasper

Wedgwood produced two major variations of Jasper: solid and dip. The solid began as a plain white body, which was then stained throughout to the desired color using coloring oxides. Wedgwood produced a number of colors over the years including more than a dozen different shades of blue and green, as well as lilac, yellow, black, white, and others. The applied relief, which had started out as a simple yet elegant white, also expanded to additional colorings. Due to rising costs of materials, the solid Jasper was removed from production and replaced with the Jasper dip process. Solid Jasper was later revived in 1854 when less expensive coloring methods were developed and has continued in production ever since.

Jasper Dip

Jasper dip was the name given to a cheaper adaptation of the original solid Jasper. Despite the initial success of the solid, a lack of cobalt oxide in the late 1700s increased production costs to the point where radical cost-cutting measures were needed. The dip process, introduced in 1777, involved dipping a plain white body into a darker colored slip. This often left a telltale uncoated base or an interior that was white. Even items that were dipped on one side, then re-dipped on another would often have exposed white edges. This dip method colored the piece utilizing less of the valuable oxide coloring and achieved almost the same effect as the solid process.

Bas-relief Ware

Wedgwood introduced Bas-relief Ware in 1817 as a less expensive imitation of Jasper dip. These items were made of lesser-quality brown clays and were then submerged in a white Jasper slip, followed by a dip in the final color. The finished product roughly simulated the look and feel of the Jasper dip. Although Bas-relief Ware utilized Jasper characteristics and decoration, the body itself was not Jasper. Close inspection inside or on the bottom of these pieces often reveals the brown coloring of the under-most layer of clay showing through. This is a sure sign that the piece is of the Bas-Relief period. For a time, both Bas-relief Ware and Jasper Dip were made concurrently. The Bas-relief was used for more common, less important items such as jugs, creamers, boxes, and other small items. The dip was reserved for the more expensive and elegant pieces such as trophy plates, vases, and large ornamental pieces.

Bas-relief Ware reduced production expenses in a variety of ways. The cheaper clay fired at lower temperatures, saving fuel costs. These wares had less spoilage in the kilns and the materials cost was far less than the Jasper dip items. Wedgwood also increased output by relaxing their imperfection tolerances. Josiah Wedgwood II approached perfection from a more economic standpoint than his father did before him. As sales slowed, Wedgwood II employed cost-cutting short cuts to keep the business going, using ingredients that were of lesser quality. However, the quality of the best Bas-relief Wares was almost indistinguishable from their dip counterparts.

Colorings of Bas-relief Wares to some extent followed the dip, with dark blue, pale blue, black, and sage green as their main colors. There have also been rumors of crimson and olive green colored Bas-Relief Ware pieces produced at the same time as the crimson and olive green Jasper dip periods. This is important because, though there is a difference between the two types of crimson, this has not detracted from their value. This informa-

tion is not well known and probably would not have any great impact on price if it was. Wedgwood also decorated some Bas-relief Wares with copper and silver, resulting in a metal surface.

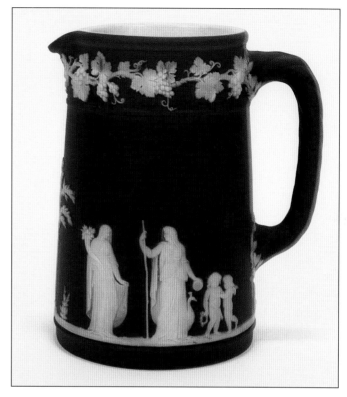

Pitcher, c. 1897-1940. Black Bas-relief, rope handled with white relief depicting *Tyche (Fortuna) with cornucopia hand, Aphrodite (Venus), Aries (Mars)*. 5.5". *Author's Collection.* $300-400.

Arms Ware was another version, consisting mainly of vase miniatures and other well-known shapes. Souvenir shops in England carried these decorated with arms or civil crests in white relief. Mounting Ware was yet another version, characterized by metal bands around the rims of pieces such as on biscuit barrels, typically using electroplated nickel silver.

Bas-relief versus Bas-Relief Ware

Two Wedgwood terms that sometimes confuse collectors are Bas-Relief and Bas-Relief Ware. Bas-Relief Ware as mentioned above refers to the pottery itself that is made to simulate Jasper and indeed has Jasper components in its make-up. Bas-Relief is the term for the applied figures and borders on the Jasper or Bas-Relief pieces. This type of relief is often thin and almost translucent, allowing the color of the body to show through slightly. Earlier, Wedgwood had utilized this method of decoration, but its delicate work requiring skilled laborers eventually proved too costly. Wedgwood later replaced this style of relief with what we see on current day Jasper. The new relief is thicker and less detailed and better suited to mass-production.

Jasper Colors

Wedgwood produced Jasper in a number of different colors since its introduction in 1774. Blue has been the dominant color in both quantity and length of time in production. Colors have also included yellow, white, grey, lilac, brown, and black, which appeared at different times depending on availability of coloring agents. One of Wedgwood's earliest signature colors was dark blue, followed later by the cobalt blue, but more recently replaced by pale blue as the dominant color in Jasper. The list of Jasper colors is lengthy and is somewhat complicated by trials and experiments with varying shades of regularly produced colors. It has been said that during the entire history of Jasper there have been many different shades of blue produced, which might include trials that never made it to the market in great quantity. Wedgwood has never formally recognized a specific number of color shades, though the evidence is clear that the possible variations are numerous.

Twentieth Century Jasper

The twentieth century saw a number of new colorings, experimental shapes, as well as designs in both dip and solid Jasper. In 1929, Wedgwood introduced buff colored Jasper with black relief (sometimes referred to as yellow-buff). This was a dip version and is considered a tri-colored Jasper item with the exposed parts of the white body offsetting the black and buff coloring. Collectors today consider this color combination very desirable, but in 1929 the color combination did not sell well and forced Wedgwood to cut production short in 1933. The shorter the time and item was produced by Wedgwood, the more valuable the item is to today's collector. Even today, the lower the quantity of the color Wedgwood produces, the more rare and desirable the piece becomes.

Crimson and Olive

Manufacturing irregularities can also influence the price and collectible nature of a desired item. Crimson Jasper, developed by Harry Barnard and Bert Bentley in 1910, is one such case. The crimson was a rich, vibrant red produced briefly in 1910 and from 1925-1932. The crimson Jasper had trouble with its strong body color bleeding through the decorative white relief. Olive Jasper dip, introduced in 1920, had the same problem. Wedgwood considered both colors failures. Today's collectors are not deterred by production difficulties with the crimson color and crimson Jasper. These two colors remains the most sought after pieces from this period as there was only a limited number produced.

A word of caution to new collectors: beware of dealers or on-line auctions that claim to be selling true crimson pieces. Wedgwood has recently begun mass-produc-

ing for the Japanese market a color of Jasper called "wine." A few of these wine Jasper items have shown up in on-line auction sites under the description of crimson (sometimes with out any mention of the word Wine), which is misleading and exploits the fact that American collectors have not been exposed to this color of Jasper through normal commercial channels. Though the wine color may have its own merits, it does not compare to the brilliance or quality of true crimson.

Vase, c. 1920. Crimson-dip, with cover.
Courtesy of the Slavid Collection.
$1,600-1,800.

There are several ways to make sure what you are buying is indeed a piece of crimson Jasper. First, the color of wine Jasper has a darker, flatter hue than the crimson, which is rich and vibrant. Determining color may be difficult via electronic photographs, thus nothing beats seeing the item in person. Second, crimson is a dipped item, thus should have some white visible on the body versus the solid color of the wine Jasper. Third, the border decorations of the wine items are a newer style that has not been produced on older Wedgwood pieces. Typically, crimson and other Jasper items of the time had border decorations that were more classical and floral in design, the wine pieces have a newer, whimsical design type. Finally, the price difference — true crimson pieces command price tags twenty-times larger than the modern day wine.

As to cautious collecting of true olive Jasper pieces, when olive dip was in production some pieces experienced an odd chemical reaction that turned parts of their relief from white to pink or tan (which further encouraged Wedgwood to discontinue the color). Some olive Jasper pieces are listed to be tri-color items, but this is false.

Unusual Jasper Colors

Royal blue Jasper was introduced in 1953 to commemorate the coronation of Queen Elizabeth II. The royal blue color has not been used at any other time. In 1957, terracotta Jasper was introduced with black or white relief. These items did not last long and were discontinued in 1959. Terracotta was later put back into production and produced on and off throughout the 1990s for specific tea and dessert wares. Bert Bentley mainly did three-color Jasper during the years of 1915-1935 such as white with green and lilac, adding a completely new dimension to the art of decorating Jasper. His more famous pieces however revolved around his work with black and white.

The Wedgwood factory has been known to create test items and colors in brief productions. Primrose Jasper was one such limited trial, produced in 1976 with a primrose yellow body and shapes decorated with a Prunis pattern. Later, Wedgwood produced a line of shapes reminiscent of the Bamboo Ware (see Cane Ware, Chapter 7) in the primrose color, decorated with terracotta colored relief. Similarly, in 1983 Wedgwood produced several small items such as pill and trinket boxes, small vases, and dishes in taupe and in teal. Both were decorated in distinctive white scalloped shell relief with no additional border decoration.

Dice Ware

Dice Ware, sometimes referred to as Dice Pattern, is a Jasper decoration technique. Its features a distinctive checkered pattern that was produced on an engine-turn-ing lathe. The checkered effect was produced by cutting through a colored dip down to the contrasting white ground at regular intervals (typically a white ground was used). Most often, a third color augmented the design and added yet another layer of intricacy. Dice Ware was difficult to produce and is considered today an expensive and rare find.

Wedgwood introduced Dice Ware in 1785, produced it for a short time, and then discontinued it due to the costly labor required to produce each piece. A short revival of this process emerged in the mid- to late nineteenth century, but in limited quantities. The shapes include vases, trophy plates, cassolettes, tobacco jars, and coffee cans decorated with trailing flowers and checkered light and dark squares with applied colored rosettes.

Vase, c. late 1700s. Dice Ware, lilac and white with green quatre-foils, missing cove. Grooves cut in the Dice Ware pattern indicate early engine-turning, indicating an earlier and higher quality piece. *Courtesy of the Slavid Collection.* $2,500-3,000.

Jasper Artists

Artist/Sculptor: John Flaxman

John Flaxman (1755-1826) was an artist and a sculptor who gained great fame for his creativity outside of his experiences with Wedgwood. His introduction to the ceramics industry came early in life, when he would accompany his father, John Flaxman Sr., in his business of molding plaster casts for various potteries including Wedgwood. The younger Flaxman's artistic skill caught the attention of Thomas Bentley who engaged Flaxman in 1775 to model Jasper items for Wedgwood. Building on this success, Flaxman struck out on his own as a sculptor and modeler working for a number of potteries in addition to Wedgwood.

Flaxman's sculpting and modeling for Wedgwood was extensive. One of Flaxman's more famous creations for Wedgwood was his Homeric Vase, modeled in 1778 in Jasper (later produced in Basalt). It was sometimes called the Pegasus Vase due to the Pegasus finial on top, but the subject that is represented in the design is the Apotheosis of Homer. Later, Flaxman modeled a companion vase in the same style and size, which he called the Apotheosis of Virgil Vase. A removable and ornately decorated Jasper base occasionally accompanied these vases.

Another famous Flaxman contribution to Wedgwood's artistry was the set of Six Muses of the Arts. Apollo was often depicted with the Muses in the scenes. Flaxman also produced a series of chess pieces of a medieval theme, which are highly sought after by collectors.

Sculptor: William Hackwood

William Hackwood was another sculptor who worked for Wedgwood from 1769-1832. He created extensive figures for Wedgwood as well as busts and portrait medallions. Among the many classical figures Hackwood modeled are the famous Dancing Hours figures, which are still in use today. The Dancing Hours figures have occasionally been attributed to John Flaxman, but this is incorrect. Flaxman did in fact create similar figures, but the molds were somehow destroyed and Hackwood had to model a replacement set. In Harry Barnard's book, *Chats on Wedgwood Ware*, he indicates that two plaques of Flaxman's original Dancing Hours designs survived, but all figures produced afterwards and through today were designed by William Hackwood in 1802. William Hackwood also worked on the Slave Medallion, which is covered in more detail later in this chapter.

Artist: Harry Barnard

Harry Barnard was a Wedgwood artist from 1862-1933 who contributed a number of innovations to the Jasper legacy. One of his most widely recognized works was his foliate pattern in raised slip that he applied free-handed to Jasper bodies. He created this radically new design using a pastry bag. Despite the perceived simplicity to his foliate patterns, the resulting beauty of his slip-trailed and applied decoration makes Barnard's creations stand out among the Jasper line. Today, his creations are high in demand as well as value.

Prominent Jasper Creations

Several distinctive shapes made a lasting impact and did a great deal towards furthering the success of the Jasper name. Two of the most significant are below, but there are many others.

King chess piece, c. 1800. White, mounted on a white circular plinth, by John Flaxman, 4 1/8". *Courtesy of the Slavid Collection.* $650-750.

Brush box, c. 1900. Cobalt blue, rectangular shaped, decorated with white foliate slip, by Harry Barnard, 6 7/8". *Courtesy of the Slavid Collection.* $950-1,000.

Slave Medallion

Wedgwood has produced many intriguing shapes and designs over the past two centuries, one such example is their Slave Medallion. Though the medallion shape is common, the story behind this particular piece and its ties to world events is unique. Its existence speaks not only to Josiah Wedgwood's attention to current events, but also to his active support of humanitarian causes.

The Slave Medallion came about during the 1700s when the slave trade came under fire in the American colonies. Wedgwood sought to help raise awareness of the movement in both England and America. Wedgwood produced an unknown quantity of these cameos in 1788. These he gave away to the supporters and members of the Society for the Abolition of the Slave Trade. Thinking correctly that abolishing slavery itself would be too large a task, the Society instead targeted the slave trade itself. They spread their message about the moral abomination and inhumane practice of buying and selling people into slavery, which at the time was a profitable business. It was the first step of its kind toward the eventual elimination of slavery in America.

The Slave Medallion was based on the seal of the "Society for the Abolition of the Slave Trade" designed and created in mid-1787. The design of the seal has historically been attributed to William Hackwood. To be more precise, the seal was designed and used by the Society for the Abolition of the Slave Trade before the Slave Medallions were produced. Hackwood, however, is the person who adapted the seal into a working cameo/intaglio for Wedgwood. The image consists of a kneeling slave figure with wrists shackled and upraised. The figure is down on one knee and underneath are the words, "Am I not a Man and a Brother?" in raised lettering. This was the first known usage of lettering in a relief design, as the process was very difficult to accomplish.

The Slave Medallion was first produced in 1788 in Black Basalt intaglios and Jasper Cameos. The original Jasper colors were black on white, though other colors appear in Wedgwood records including white on yellow, white on dark blue, black on yellow, and white on black.

It has been said that Wedgwood himself shipped a number of these to friends in America, including a large number to Benjamin Franklin for his friends and fellow supporters. These early pieces do not have any Wedgwood marks, probably because the expense to hand stamp them was not economically reasonable for a "give-away" item.

A term that is sometimes used out of context is "Slave Medallion." The proper name for the slave design itself is the "Seal of the Society for the Abolition of the Slave Trade" (In Robin Reilly's Dictionary, *The Wedgwood New Illustrated Dictionary*, he refers to it as the "Slave Emancipation Society Seal.") This is important when describing the image, particularly when it shows up on different ceramic bodies, including Jasper pin dishes, Jasper desert plates, and Jasper jugs. The term "Slave Medallion" refers specifically to the medallion shape decorated with the Seal.

Slave Medallion, 1975-1976. White with black relief, reproduction commissioned by the Buten Museum. *Courtesy of the Frazier Collection.* $150-200.

Portland Vase

Of all the shapes and vases that Wedgwood produced, the one that marks the high point of the Jasper evolution was Josiah Wedgwood's creation of the Portland Vase. Wedgwood first introduced the Portland Vase in 1790. Today the Portland Vase shape has been incorporated into the company's logo and represents the Wedgwood company itself.

The Portland vase was an exact replica of the famous blue-glass Barbarini Vase. A great deal has been written on this subject of the Portland Vase and Wolf Mankowitz (as well as others) wrote entire books on the subject, which are considered very thorough accounts of its origins.

The Barbarini Vase was made of cameo glass with white enamel relief. Its age is not known for certain, but it is believed to date back to the Romans. Wedgwood encountered the vase in 1786. The Duke of Portland loaned the vase to Josiah Wedgwood to study. He worked for years on the shape, texture, and color and in 1789 completed what has been regarded as his life's masterpiece. Numerous advance orders were taken for the impending work of art, which Wedgwood completed in 1789, a perfect Jasper replica of the blue and white glass vase. The total number of this first run is unknown.

Numbers of subsequent editions in various colors and sizes of the Portland Vase were produced off and on for the next two centuries.

Evaluating a Portland Vase by quality can help narrow down a production period, if one knows what to look for. The relief can characterize the Portland Vases of the first release period. The details on the figures should be sharp and defined and the relief should also be thin and delicate, almost translucent. Twentieth century vases will have thicker, opaque relief and the details will be less crisp. Cheaper, non-Wedgwood copies will sometimes be molded as one piece, without hand-applied ornament and the colors will have been painted on. If you come across one of these through a cluttered antique shop window, you might not be able to discern the difference, as I once did. However, once you are within a few feet of it, there should be no question that it is not a Wedgwood product.

Bowing to prudish trends, the Wedgwood company produced a brief line of Portland Vases in 1839 with draped figures. Modesty had the center of attention in the art world at that time, so Wedgwood complied with its customers' requests. In subsequent editions, the Portland Vase figures were generally returned to their original state.

In 1877, Wedgwood co-produced a limited edition of fifteen Portland Vases with a glass manufacturer by the name of John Northwood. Business and labor was stretched so thin that Wedgwood outsourced some of the workload. At his company, the Stourbridge Glass Works, Northwood completed the final polishing steps on these Portland Vases using a lapidary wheel. Each vase was marked with a "JN" and a triangle mark at the base of the tree relief on the vase body indicating Northwood's involvement. These became known as the Northwood Portland Vases.

In 1919, Bert Bentley and Harry Barnard collectively introduced a new edition of the Portland Vase. A Royal Blue colored version was produced for a limited time in 1953 as part of Wedgwood's line to celebrate the coronation of Queen Elizabeth. It should be noted that the royal color has always been reserved exclusively for events involving the English Royalty. A new limited edition was produced in 1980 to commemorate the 250th birthday of Josiah Wedgwood. Finally, the most recent know limited edition of Portland Vases to be produced were in 1989, commemorating the 200th anniversary of Josiah Wedgwood's perfecting the Portland Vase.

Portland Vase, c. mid-1800s. Cobalt blue Jasper Dip with draped relief in white, 5". *Author's Collection.* $600-800.

Three items with relief depicting *Marriage of Cupid and Psyche.* (Left) Medallion, c. 1920, blue and white Jasper by Burt Bentley, $400-600. (Center) Non-Wedgwood wax copy, c. 1780, from the Marlbough gem of the same cupid image, $600-800. (Right) Medallion, c. 1775, blue and white, set in frame (Wedgwood & Bentley mark), $800-1,000. *Courtesy of the Horn and Hoffman Collection.*

Three medallions in celebration of King George III recovering his health, modeled by Edward Burch. (Left) Blue and white Jasper, c. 1785, $400-600. (Center) Basalt in oval box, c. 1789, $400-600. (Right) Blue and white Jasper, c. 1779, with crown above the portrait and a ribbon that reads "Health Restored," $400-600. *Courtesy of the Horn and Hoffman Collection.*

Pair of cups and saucers, c. 1780. Dice Ware, blue and white with gold florets and grooves from engine turning. *Courtesy of the Slavid Collection.* $5,500-6,500.

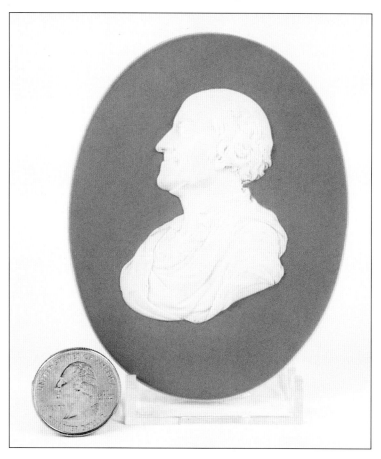

Medallion, c. 1778. White on lilac depicting *Voltaire*, with polished edges, modeled by W. Hackwood. 3.25" x 4". *Courtesy of the Chellis and Adams Collection.* $700-800.

Medallion, c. 1782-1788. Blue and white, framed with relief depicting *Frederica Sophia Wilholmina of Orange.* She was a Prussian princess married to William V of Orange, born 1751, died 1820. (Features Wedgwood mark plus two firing holes in back). *Courtesy of the Horn and Hoffman Collection.* $400-600.

King chess piece, c. 1785. White with lilac base, modeled by John Flaxman. *Courtesy of the Horn and Hoffman Collection.* $550-600.

Pair of patch boxes/sewing kits, c. 1785-1790. Jasper set in ivory, with metal hinged boxes, 3.5" x 1". *Courtesy of the Chellis and Adams Collectio.* $400-500 each.

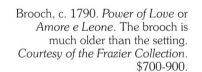

Brooch, c. 1790. *Power of Love* or *Amore e Leone*. The brooch is much older than the setting. *Courtesy of the Frazier Collection.* $700-900.

Wax portrait of Alexander the Great modeled and signed by John Flaxman (non-Wedgwood), c. 1779, $500-800. Medallion modeled by John Flaxman, c. 1820, $300-500. *Courtesy of the Horn and Hoffman Collection.*

141

Cup (a.k.a. "can"), c. 1790. Dice Ware tri-colored dip, blue and white with applied yellow quatrefoils and running white laurel borders. *Courtesy of the Frazier Collection.* $1,200-1,300.

White on Black Jasper medallion of Admiral Howe by Burt Bentley, c. 1920, $400-600. White glass paste, c. 1798, by James Tassie (non-Wedgwood), also depicting Admiral Howe. *Courtesy of the Horn and Hoffman Collection.* $300-500.

Two miniature oval three-color Jasper pieces with scene depicting *Sacrifice to Diana*. (Top) blue, green, white, c. 1780-1790. (Bottom) black, yellow, white, c. 1786-1790. *Courtesy of the Horn and Hoffman Collection.* $300-350 each.

Two medallions depicting Sir Isaac Newton with the comet he discovered. Jasper self-framed medallion, c. 1800, $400-600. Basalt medallion, c. 1800, $500-700. *Courtesy of the Horn and Hoffman Collection.*

Medallion, c. 1800. Dark Blue and white, set into a cut steel belt buckle with polished edge and multifaceted back in a red leather oval box. Attributed to Matthew Boulton. *Courtesy of the Slavid Collection.* $1,250.

Jester or *Fool* chess piece, c. 1800. White mounted on white plinth, by John Flaxman. The *Jester* piece was made for the French market, first ordered in 1783. The French chess enthusiasts replaced the *Bishop* chess piece with *Le Fou* (the Fool). *Courtesy of the Slavid Collection.* $850.

Oil lamp, 1800-1850. Green-dip and *Dancing Hours* relief. This particular lamp includes a glass hurricane cylinder, globe, and wick unit. The oil staining on the body denotes that this piece has been used as an oil lamp. *Courtesy of the Frazier Collection*. $1,000-1,200.

Locket, 1800-1810. Features *Hope* relief, mounting is newer than the age of the medallion. *Courtesy of the Frazier Collection*. $150-200.

Tablet, c. 1800-1820. Green jasper dip with white relief, depicting *Seven ages of man*, 25" x 10". Marked just Wedgwood. *Courtesy of the Chellis and Adams Collection.* $3,000-4,000.

Medallion, c. 1800. Depicts Italian Poet Dante Alighieri (1265-1321). His most famous work was *La Divine Commedia* (*Divine Comedy*), common in prints but very rare in medallions. *Courtesy of the Horn and Hoffman Collection.* $600-800.

Three portrait medallions. (Left) white on green Jasper, depicting Adam Smith, c. 1820. (Center) Depicting Townley, deeply molded, c. 1800. (Right) Green and white, with relief depicting Sir Joseph Banks (Rowland Hill mark), c. 1800. *Courtesy of the Horn and Hoffman Collection.* $300-500 each.

147

White on blue Jasper medallion, c. 1920, depicting Peter the Great of Russia by Burt Bentley. White smear-glazed stoneware medallion, c. 1800, also of Peter the Great of Russia. *Courtesy of the Horn and Hoffman Collection.* $300-500 each.

Tablet, c. 1820. Sage green with white relief depicting *Achilles Dragging Hector around the walls of Troy*, 18" x 6" not including the wood frame. *Courtesy of the Chellis and Adams Collection.* $2,500-3,500.

White on Blue Jasper Medallion, c. 1800, depicting Dr. Joseph Priestly, chemist friend of Josiah Wedgwood and a member of the Luna Society, $300-500. White smear-glazed stoneware bin-marker, c. early 1800s, of Dr. Joseph Priestly. *Courtesy of the Horn and Hoffman Collection.* $200-400.

Two white and blue portrait medallions depicting the *Three Graces*. Lapidary polished surface, c. 1800, $300-500. White and blue oil lamp cover depicting of the *Three Graces*, c. 1820. *Courtesy of the Horn and Hoffman Collection.* $300-500.

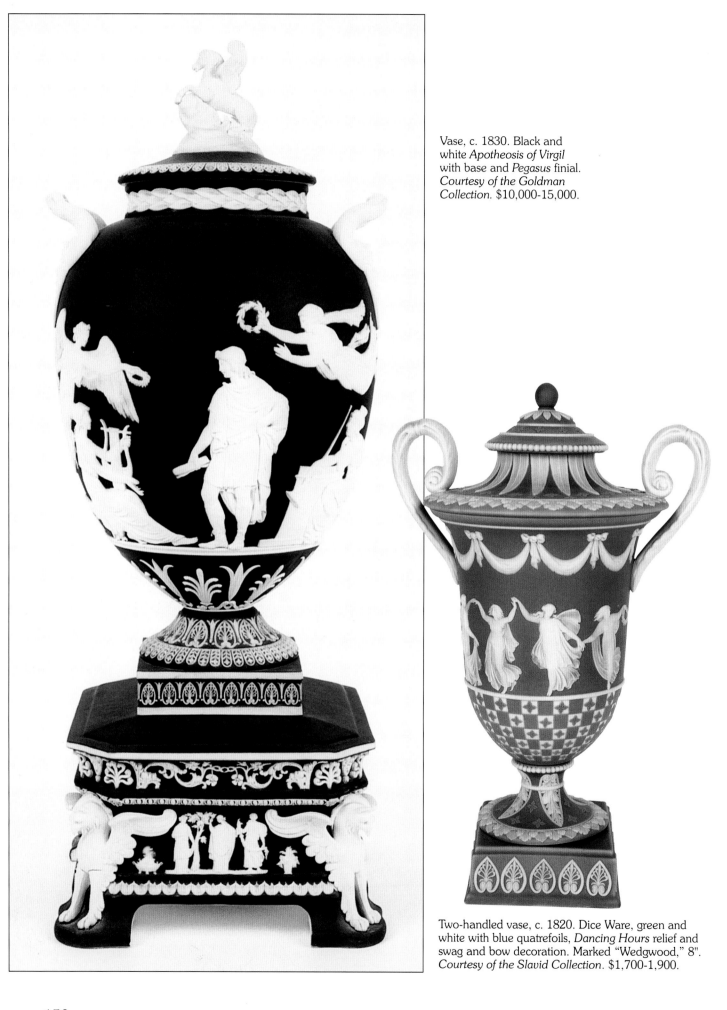

Vase, c. 1830. Black and white *Apotheosis of Virgil* with base and *Pegasus* finial. *Courtesy of the Goldman Collection.* $10,000-15,000.

Two-handled vase, c. 1820. Dice Ware, green and white with blue quatrefoils, *Dancing Hours* relief and swag and bow decoration. Marked "Wedgwood," 8". *Courtesy of the Slavid Collection.* $1,700-1,900.

150

Tablet, c. mid-1800s. Tri-color, green with blue border and white relief depicting *Offering to Peace*, 4" x 11". *Courtesy of the Goldman Collection.* $900-1,200.

Bonsai pot, c. 1840. Cobalt-dip with drain-hole in the bottom, 2". *Courtesy of the Frazier Collection.* $75-150.

Rectangular portrait medallion, c. 1860. Depicts Francis Palgrave. *Courtesy of the Horn and Hoffman Collection.* $400-500.

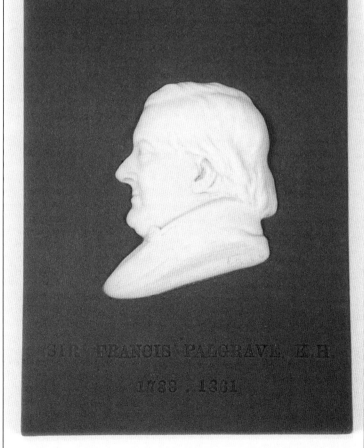

Portland Vase (full size), c. 1800s. Cobalt blue dip with undraped white bas-relief figures and Paris Cap on bottom. Mark: "WEDGWOOD." *Courtesy of the Chellis and Adams Collection.* $2,200-2,800.

Pair of coffee cans and saucers, c. 1870 .Tri-colored with festoons and ornate decorations. *Courtesy of the Goldman Collection.* $600-800 each.

Coffee pot with cover, c. 1872. Sage green with white relief depicting *Sacrifice to Ceres* and grape leaf border, 8.5". *Courtesy of the Frazier Collection.* $250-300.

Tobacco Pipe, 1875. Cobalt blue dip with white relief. Has removable moisture trap and original stem. Marks: impressed "Staite's Patent." *Courtesy of the Frazier Collection.* $225-500.

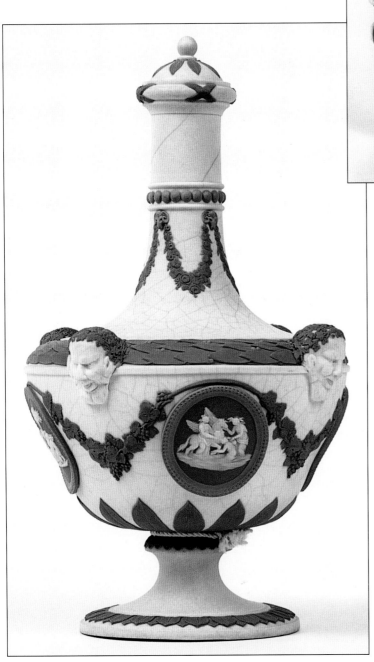

Barber Bottle, 1867. Tri-colored with white, green, and lilac relief, surface has slight surface crackle, 10" (TWV mark). *Courtesy of the Frazier Collection.* $1,300-1,400.

Vase, c. mid-1800s. Lilac and white covered vase with dove finial. Marked "Wedgwood." *Courtesy of the Slavid Collection.* $950-1,000.

Vase, 1868. Pale blue and white with a single handle, flower and reed design, (WUR mark), 8". *Courtesy of the Slavid Collection.* $1,200-1,800.

Vase, c. 1875-1885. Four-color with green, yellow, white, and lilac, decorated with Monopodia (masks) of lion heads and floral swags. *Courtesy of the Slavid Collection.* $1,400.

Rectangular medallion, c. 1800s. Black with crest relief consisting of two torches crossed – French and American Statue of Liberty torches, 2.5" x 3.5". *Courtesy of the Chellis and Adams Collection.* $400-600.

Vase, c. 1800s. Pale green-dip with white relief depicting *Hercules in the Garden of the Hesperides*. Has handles, but is missing its cover, (WEDGWOOD mark). *Courtesy of the Chellis and Adams Collection.* $850-1,000.

Perfume bottle,
c. 1800s. Cobalt blue,
silver top and flat
bottom (it is rare to find
early perfume bottles
with flat bottoms), 3.5"
(Wedgwood mark).
*Courtesy of the Slavid
Collection.* $400-450.

Mini-jug, c. 1880. Cobalt blue and white with
Satyr mask below its single handle, 4".
Courtesy of the Slavid Collection. $200-300.

Perfume bottle, reverse side.
Courtesy of the Slavid Collection.

Two cobalt blue Jasper dip pieces, c. 1891-1897. (Left) spill vase *Author's Collection,* (right) small rope-handled jug. *Courtesy of the Milan Collection.* $100-140 each.

Etruscan jug, c. 1890-1897. Olive green-dip with white relief of *Nike the Warrior,* 4.25". *Author's Collection.* $70-90.

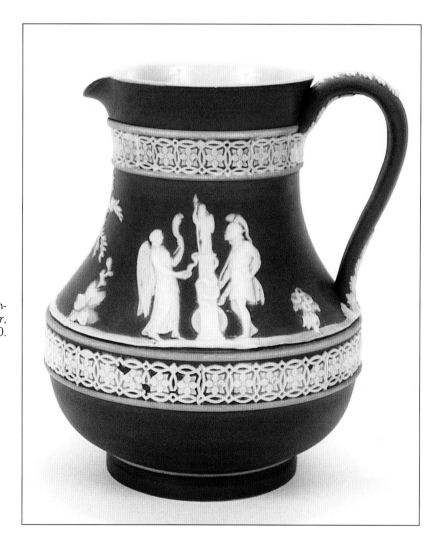

Tea Canister, 1891. Pale green
dip with white bas-relief.
*Courtesy of the Frazier
Collection.* $150-250.

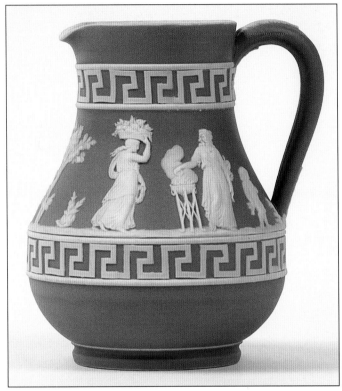

Etruscan Jug, 1891. Lilac dip with white bas-relief
representing *Sacrifice to Ceres* with Greek Key borders,
6.5". *Courtesy of the Frazier Collection.* $250-300.

Jug, c. 1890. Orange shape,
olive green-dip with white
bas-relief depicting *Apollo*
with lyre, 6". *Courtesy of the
Frazier Collection.* $200-300.

160

Plaque, c. 1800s. Blue, white, and green *Cupid with Psyche* design, 5.5" x 17.5". *Courtesy of the Slavid Collection.* $2,000-2,500.

Covered mini chocolate pot, c. 1890. Blue, buff (yellow), and white with *Watering Pegasus* relief, 3.5". *Courtesy of the Slavid Collection.* $1,000.

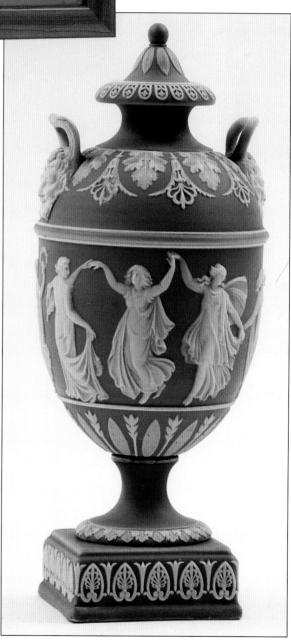

Covered vase with Bacchus head handles, c. late 1800s. Pale green dip with white relief depicting the *Dancing Hours* figures and foliate borders. Mark: "WEDGWOOD." *Courtesy of the Chellis and Adams Collection.* $700-900.

Pair of oversized medallions, c. 1902 . Black and white, (left) relief of Queen
Alexandra and (right) relief of Edward VII, modeled by Watkin, 8.5".
Courtesy of the Horn and Hoffman Collection. Pair: $800-1,000.

Compact, c. mid-1900s. Inlaid pale blue medallion with *Three
Graces* relief. *Courtesy of the Milan Collection.* $90-100.

162

Wall Plaque, c. early 1900s. Pale blue Jasper with white relief depicting *Dancing Hours* figures. *Courtesy of the Chellis and Adams Collection.* $600-700.

Portland Vase, c. early 1900s. Solid black with white relief. *Courtesy of the Frazier Collection.* $450-600.

Heart box, 1910-1928. Crimson-dip with white relief depicting *Icarus and Daedalus*. *Courtesy of the Frazier Collection*. $900-1,200.

Vase, c. 1910. Buff (yellow) dip with black bas-relief depicting *Nike and Warrior*, 5.125". *Courtesy of the Frazier Collection*. $325-375.

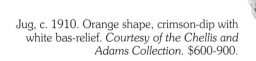

Jug, c. 1910. Orange shape, crimson-dip with white bas-relief. *Courtesy of the Chellis and Adams Collection*. $600-900.

Square box, 1910-1928. Crimson-dip with white bas-relief depicting *Sportive Love. Courtesy of the Frazier Collection.* $1,100-1,400.

Medallion, c. 1919. World War I Peace Medallions presented to Wedgwood workers who had served in the war. Mounted and framed, black and white Jasper, reads, "Justice and Liberty 1914-1919." *Courtesy of the Horn and Hoffman Collection.* $500-700.

Chamber stick, c. 1920. Dark olive green dip. *Courtesy of the Frazier Collection.* $150-200.

Jardinière, c. 1920. Chrome green-dip Bas-Relief Ware with white bas-relief of Muses, lion heads, and garlands, 9 1/8". *Courtesy of the Frazier Collection.* $500-650.

Teapot with cover, c. 1920. Olive with white bas-relief. *Courtesy of the Frazier Collection.* $75-125.

Sugar bowl with cover, c. 1920. Olive with white bas-relief.
Courtesy of the Frazier Collection. $50-100.

Biscuit barrel, 1923-1933.
Buff-dip with black relief of
floral swags and lion heads
stainless steel handle and
rim. *Author's Collection.*
$750-950.

167

Salt & Pepper shakers, 1955. "Imperial" shape, sage-green and white. *Courtesy of the Frazier Collection.* $60-80.

Posey pot, c. 1930. White on cobalt blue with acanthus leaf design and "buttonwood" or daisy design, glazed interior, 4 1/16". *Courtesy of the Frazier Collection.* $75-150.

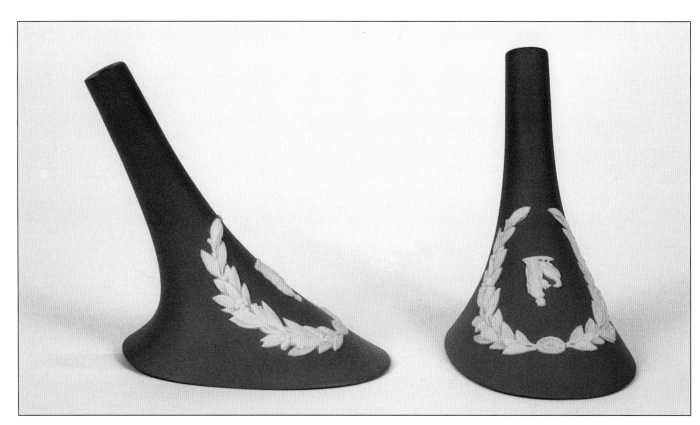

Pair of women's shoe heels, c. 1950. Sage Green, un-mounted with white relief depicting *Hebe and the Eagle. Courtesy of the Horn and Hoffman Collection.* $250-300.

168

Dessert plate, c. 1900s. Green with terracotta horse reliefs after Stubbs' horse study, 6.5". *Author's Collection*. $50-55.

Urn, c. 1955-1960. Black and white with square plinth, *Dancing Hours* relief and acorn finial. *Courtesy of the Slavid Collection*. $700-900.

Knob boxes. Three round boxes with white grapevine border and spike tops. (Left) lilac, 3", c. 1960s. *Courtesy of the Milan Collection*. $40-50. (Center) Pale blue, 5". c 1962. *Author's Collection*. $75-100. (Right) Pale blue, 3". *Author's Collection*. $30-40.

Vase, c. 1970s. Pale blue with festoons, lion heads, and muse reliefs, 6". *Author's Collection*. $65-75.

Trophy Plate, 1960. Lilac with white bas-relief depicting *Muses Watering Pegasus*, 8.75". *Courtesy of the Frazier Collection*. $550-650.

Wedgwood sample plaque used to showcase different Jasper colors, c. 1900s. Features thirteen colored medallions (three black, three green, two lilac, five blue) mounted on white Jasper. *Courtesy of the Slavid Collection*. $1,200-1,500.

Bowl, c. 1965. Black with white Arabesque relief, with acanthus and oak leaves. *Courtesy of the Frazier Collection.* $400-500.

Sweet dish, c. 1975. White with green relief depicting Irish harp and shamrock border, 4.5". *Courtesy of the Frazier Collection.* $35-55.

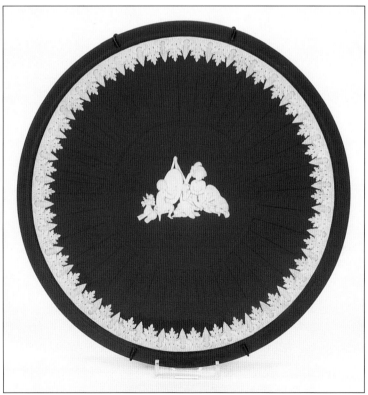

Cake Plate, 1975-1976. Fluted design, Portland blue with white relief depicting *Infant Academy*, design by Joshua Reynolds (original design c. 1790), 10.25". *Courtesy of the Frazier Collection.* $150-250.

Canopic Jar, 1976. Black and terracotta with
Zodiac symbols and hieroglyphs in relief.
Courtesy of the Slavid Collection. $800-1,000.

Tri-colored medallion, 1977. Lilac, blue, and white
with relief depicting the *Three Graces*, 1.5".
Courtesy of the Frazier Collection. $50-75.

Bowl, 1976. Primrose Jasper
with white Prunus relief.
Author's Collection. $70-90.

Canopic Jar, c. 1978. Terracotta on primrose with
Zodiac symbols and hieroglyphs in relief, 9.5".
Courtesy of the Slavid Collection. $800-1,000.

Bud vase, 1978. Square shaped design, black
and terracotta, Egyptian-styled relief, 5.5".
Courtesy of the Frazier Collection. $75-100.

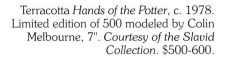

Terracotta *Hands of the Potter*, c. 1978.
Limited edition of 500 modeled by Colin
Melbourne, 7". *Courtesy of the Slavid
Collection.* $500-600.

Pair of candlesticks, 1980. Lilac with white relief, 4.75".
Courtesy of the Frazier Collection. $175-225.

Bud vase, 1978. Square shaped design,
terracotta on primrose, trial piece, only fifty
were made. Egyptian relief including griffin,
bird, and palm motifs. *Courtesy of the
Frazier Collection.* $250-275.

Vase, c. 1979. Primrose with
terracotta, bamboo-shape. *Courtesy
of the Frazier Collection.* $175-250.

Four egg cups, 1992. Black, primrose, terracotta, and lilac, all with white *Dancing Hours* relief. Each: $15-20. Two egg shaped boxes, c. 1970s. Portland blue and primrose, both with white *Dancing Hours* relief. *Author's Collection.* $30-40 each.

Medallion, c. 1980s. Terra cotta with black relief, marks "AW" and "made in England." Black jasper of Medusa or Mercury. *Courtesy of the Chellis and Adams Collection.* $40-45.

Collection of playing card, symbol-shaped objects. Top row, three boxes: (Left) diamond shape, white with primrose muse relief, c. 1980s, *Author's Collection*. (Center) Portland blue spade shape, white muse relief, c. 1980s, *Courtesy of the Milan Collection*. (Right) club shape, white with lilac muse relief, c. 1980s, *Courtesy of the Milan Collection*. Each: $50-75. Bottom row, five sweet dishes with muse relief, c. 1980s: (Left to right) Portland blue heart shape, lilac spade shape, pale blue club shape, terracotta spade shape, sage green diamond shape. *Author's Collection*. Each: $25-35.

Oval tray, c. 1982. Pink with white relief depicting *Psyche bound and wounded by Cupid*, with grape leaf border, 9 7/8". *Courtesy of the Frazier Collection*. $150-200.

Bud vase, 1983. Square shaped, pink with bee and acanthus leaf design, 5.25". *Courtesy of the Frazier Collection.* $100-125.

Dessert plate, 1984. Black with straw colored Jasper relief of Arthur Guinness, numbered 5708. This was a limited edition promotion celebrating the 225th anniversary of the Guinness Company, 6.5". *Author's Collection.* $75-90.

Seven Taupe colored items with white scallop shell relief. Jasper in this color was only produced for a brief time in 1983. (Left to right) Dessert plate, 6", $35-45. Scallop edged box, $30-40. Square bud vase, $45-55. Etruscan jug, $80-100. Pear shaped vase, $45-55. Small oval box, $25-30. Round sweet dish, $25-30. *Author's Collection.*

Sacrifice Bowl, 1984. Teal with white relief. *Courtesy of the Frazier Collection*. $375-500.

Glenfiddich decanter, 1987. Special edition, pale blue with white deer relief. Decanter is filled with twenty-one-year-old scotch and is still sealed. *Author's Collection*. $450-500.

Christening spoon, c. 1984. Teal with white relief, 3 5/8".
Courtesy of the Frazier Collection. $40-60.

Right:
Dessert plate, 1986-1987. Black with white relief depicting the America's Cup Trophy. This piece was a limited edition issued to commemorate the America's Cup race, $70-85. Sweet dish, 1986-1987, pale blue with white relief of an America's Cup yacht, $30-45. *Author's Collection*.

Valentine Plate, 1985. Gray with pink relief.
Courtesy of the Frazier Collection. $35-75.

Eight demitasse cups and saucers, 1993. Relief depicting the *Dancing Hours* figures. Colors include green, Portland blue, terracotta, pink, black, primrose, lilac, pale blue. The first six were sold as a set. The green and pink pieces were sold separately. *Author's Collection*. $65-75 each.

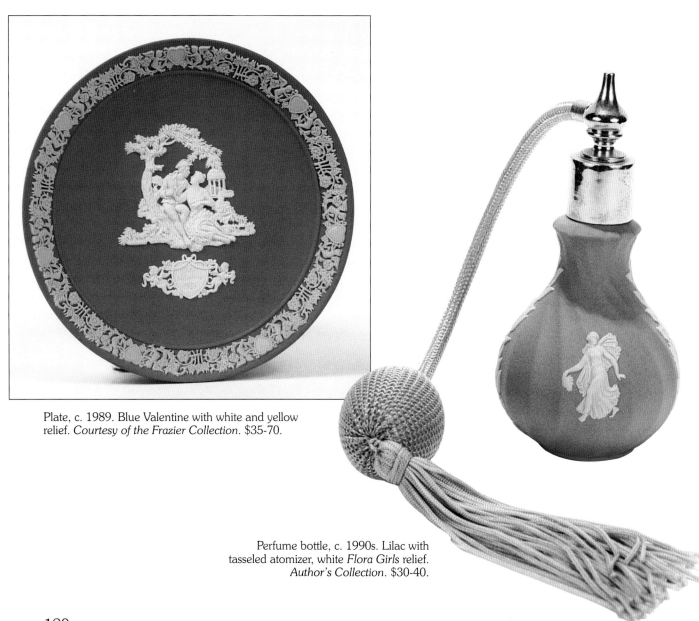

Plate, c. 1989. Blue Valentine with white and yellow relief. *Courtesy of the Frazier Collection*. $35-70.

Perfume bottle, c. 1990s. Lilac with tasseled atomizer, white *Flora Girls* relief. *Author's Collection*. $30-40.

Potpourri holder, c. 1990. Terracotta color with white muse relief and a pierced lid. *Courtesy of the Frazier Collection.* $65-85.

Humidor jar, 1990. Grey with white relief depicting *Sacrifice to Peace* and a grapevine border, 6.75". *Author's Collection.* $180-200.

Jug, 1990. Grey with white relief of *Diana with Stag* and grapevine borders, 6". *Courtesy of the Keefe Collection.* $180-200.

Bookend, c. 1990. Lion figure, black with cane colored Jasper relief, 5.25". *Courtesy of the Frazier Collection.* $125-150.

Small pitcher, c. 1990s. Black with white relief depicting *Icarus and Daedalus. Courtesy of the Keefe Collection.* $40-60.

Bud vase, 1990. Grey with white relief depicting two of the *Seasons,* one on each side, 5.5". *Courtesy of the Keefe Collection.* $50-65.

Pitcher, c. 1990s. Portland blue in the Brewster shape with rope handle. *Courtesy of the Keefe Collection.* $45-65.

Cufflinks, c. 1990-1994. Speckled Portland blue and pale blue with white ship relief and gold setting. *Author's Collection.* $100-120.

Etruscan Jug, 1997. Black with terracotta relief. *Author's Collection.* $85-95.

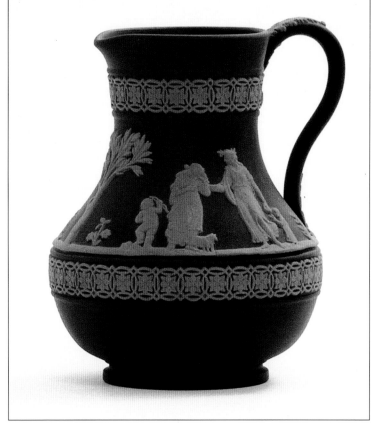

Pair of large medallions, c. 1993. Sage green with white relief depicting modified *Dancing Hours* figures. *Courtesy of the Frazier Collection.* $90-110.

Dessert plate, c. late 1900s. Pink with white *Autumn* relief. One of four reliefs depicting the lessons of life, sculpted by John Gregory for the Huntington Mausoleum. This was a commemorative piece for the 75th anniversary of the Huntington Library, 6.5". *Author's Collection.* $45-65.

Spill Vase, c. 2002. Marbleized Portland blue, pale blue, and white, 4.25". *Courtesy of the Frazier Collection.* $125-175.

Sweet dish, 2002. Heart shaped, wine colored with white relief. *Courtesy of the Frazier Collection*. $35-60.

Six cane-colored Jasper items, c. 1990s, with *Bacchanalian Boys at Play* design and black painted highlights in a style reminiscent of Cane Bamboo Ware. (Left to right) Bread & butter plate, $60-70, sugar pot with cover, $40-55, teapot, $65-75, creamer, $35-45, honey pot, $40-55, dessert plate, $50-60. *Author's Collection*.

Chapter 7
Other Dry-Body Stoneware

Although Black Basalt and Jasper are the more recognized types of dry-body Stoneware, several others have played an important role in Wedgwood's company history. These other types of dry-body Stoneware began as common, everyday wares that were simple in design and produced by nearly every Staffordshire potter. Prior to the revolutionary advances in Creamware, Stoneware served an important function during the eighteenth century as ordinary wares for day-to-day use. They required no harmful lead glazes to make their surfaces resistant to heat and liquids and the abundant local clays made these ordinary wares inexpensive and appealing to the working-class.

Like their competitors, Wedgwood also produced these wares, which at the time represented the lifeblood of the pottery industry. Never satisfied with the generic or mainstream, Josiah Wedgwood endeavored to improve these common wares in quality as well as inject a fresh and artistic design into them. His success with these other types of dry-bodied Stoneware would allow him to support his company financially while experimenting and perfecting his more expensive ornamental wares.

Dry-Body Stoneware: Rosso Antico

In the 1700s, potters in Europe were producing red Stoneware and imitating Chinese wares from Yi-hsing, China. Yi-hsing was a town on the Yangtze River in China where the Chinese had developed and produced unglazed red and brown Stoneware since the early 1500s. German, Dutch, and English potters copied and modified these Chinese wares for the European ceramics market. Europeans were attracted to their distinctive colors, decorations, and ability to withstand higher cooking temperatures than what the European potters of the time could produce.

Doric Jug with pewter top, 1871. Satyr mask below the spout, 6.5" (CKZ mark). *Author's Collection.* $500-600.

These "red wares" were primarily useful items rather than intricately decorated works. They included basic shapes like teapots, jugs, coffee pots, and other everyday kitchen items. Many different potters produced "red china," as they called it, since it was more profitable than importing the red wares from China. These red wares became common staples in most English potters' product lines with shapes and ornamentation varying little from potter to potter.

Coffee pot, c. early 1800s. Rosso Antico with enameled Famille Rose style decorations. Mark: "WEDGWOOD." *Courtesy of the Chellis and Adams Collection. $500-650.*

Josiah begrudgingly produced red ware, utilizing simple techniques he had learned during his time with Thomas Whieldon. Wedgwood disliked the red despite its popularity and prompts from his partner, Thomas Bentley, to increase its production. He wrote to Bentley, *"If it had never been made in Tpots & the commonest wares, my objection would not have existed."* This attitude may explain why he did not give appropriate attention to the quality of the early red Stoneware and why it never reached a level or style befitting of the Wedgwood name. The early red lacked the fine textures and richness in color of their competitors' wares. For a time, the red satisfied consumer demand and kept Wedgwood in business while sales on the more expensive wares, such as his Basalts, remained sluggish. After a while, the red's waning quality compared to its competitors caused interest to drop off and forced Wedgwood to discontinue it.

Not many examples of red ware early pieces survive today. For those that did survive, it is difficult to confirm their origins. Markings on the early red wares were not typical of the markings on other Wedgwood products. Most items were unmarked or marked with simulated Chinese symbols, augmented with a "W." Due to the nature of these items and their level of quality, Wedgwood was not interested in associating the company name to pieces.

Realizing there was still a strong consumer demand for red and not wanting to alienate his customers or miss a growing market segment, Wedgwood began experimenting to bring back an improved version. He refined his earlier red formula and, in 1776, introduced "Rosso Antico," which translates into "antique red." This new and improved red, which was actually closer to orange-red, exhibited a richer color, smoother texture, and allowed more creative decorations than Wedgwood's earlier red wares. Rosso Antico varied in color between brick red and chocolate, with applied decorations in black or white.

Rosso Antico's success diminished the failure of his earlier red ware, maintaining a level of quality befitting of the company's reputation. The Rosso Antico line was greatly expanded by Josiah Wedgwood II, who took over after his father's death. Wedgwood continued to produce Rosso Antico until 1900, when the popularity of Jasper eclipsed all of Wedgwood's other Stonewares.

Egyptian Influenced Rosso Antico

For collectors, history itself can often provide insight into particular designs and help determine the age of a Wedgwood piece. World events and fashion trends can provide information why a certain style or motif was introduced to the market. Egyptian styled pieces are one such category that followed the news of the day.

Though Egyptian motifs had been widely used on Black Basalt at various times in Wedgwood's history, they were also used in other ceramic bodies with success. In 1805, Wedgwood produced a line of Rosso Antico items decorated with black Egyptian-styled relief. This represented a break into new creative directions, getting away from the Oriental themes that had dominated the other red wares. It also helped Rosso Antico differentiate itself from its earlier, more mundane red ware predecessors.

Looking through history, we see influential events that drove an interest in all things Egyptian. Napoleon's 1798 invasion into Egypt, and Lord Nelson's victory over the French at the Nile in 1798, followed by his subsequent victory over the French fleet at Trafalgar in 1805, and the Rosetta Stone discovery in 1799. These events resulted in an influx of Egyptian artifacts into Europe and England, fostering a revival of interest in Ancient Egyptian art. Wedgwood was quick to capitalize on this new trend through Black Basalt and the new Rosso Antico.

Though Egyptian designs on Wedgwood date back to the Wedgwood-Bentley catalogue of 1779, early productions were limited in scope since little factual evidence was known at this time about ancient Egyptian art. Ever since Egypt came under Islamic rule in 640 A.D., travel to Egypt by Europeans was discouraged. The earliest Wedgwood pieces therefore consisted of a limited range of Egyptian designs derived from material acquired from secondary sources. In retrospect, Wedgwood's designs were not always accurate reproductions of actual Egyptian artifacts.

Plate, c. mid-1800s. Rosso Antico with black jasper Egyptian motif. *Courtesy of the Chellis and Adams Collection.* $450-500.

With only limited available information on ancient Egyptian artifacts, Wedgwood artists utilized creative license in filling the informational gaps with their classical sensibilities. This resulted in a classical interpretation of Egyptian art with subtle Greek and Roman perspectives. Despite increasing influxes of ancient Egyptian artifacts, history has shown that Wedgwood never corrected any of their inaccuracies in later editions and the hybrid interpretations remain even in the most recent Egyptian collection of 1978.

Images and figures of sphinxes, Egyptian lions, and mythological deities were common themes used by Wedgwood, as were their intricate borders, Egyptian fret, and lotus papyrus motifs. The fret is a reoccurring geometric pattern of interlocking angled lines, sometimes referred to as Greek Key. The difference between the two lies in that the Greek Key lines never actually connect, allowing their pattern to continue indefinitely. The lotus and papyrus were plant designs, which represented Upper Egypt and Lower Egypt, respectively, and their combination symbolized the unity of the two. This period also saw some of the more famous of the Rosso Antico creations, including teapots adorned with alligator finials and the first-ever Egyptian hieroglyphs on

Wedgwood wares. Aesthetics drove this early use of hieroglyphics as a form of decoration, but held little meaning for those purchasing them. No one had yet deciphered their meanings, prior to the discovery and analysis of the Rosetta Stone. Only after the Rosetta Stone was studied and analyzed were historians able to attach any meaning to these symbols.

King Tutankhamen's tomb was discovered in Egypt in 1923, which later gave way to the King Tut World Museum Tour in 1978. These events once again spurred worldwide interest and additional Wedgwood lines of Egyptian-influenced items followed. This included items similar to the older, Rosso Antico shapes, but made from terracotta and black Jasper, terracotta and primrose Jasper, and in gilded basalts. Shapes included Sphinx figures and canopic jars reminiscent of similar items produced by Wedgwood in Black Basalt during the eighteenth century. Most Egyptian-styled Wedgwood in the market today is from this period. Rosso Antico items are rarer and predate this production.

Rosso Antico: Cambridge Ale Jug

A simpler, more common shape associated with the Rosso Antico name is the Cambridge Ale jug, introduced in 1859. These were not nearly as intricate as the Egyptian Rosso Antico wares, as they were more utilitarian in nature and illustrate Wedgwood's attempt to cover both the artistic and the day-to-day sides of the ceramics business.

Small Cambridge Ale jug, c. 1890s. Rosso Antico. Marks: "WEDGWOOD, ENGLAND," printed: "Cambridge Ale Jug, Sold by Woollard & Co.", 4.25". *Author's Collection.* $70-80.

These Cambridge Ale jugs have a distinctive bulbous shaped bottom, and then are tapered upwards until their very pronounced rimmed spout. Some jugs were undecorated; some had inlaid decoration in the Henry II style. The Henry II style refers to a method of indented design, similar to intaglio, which is then filled with colored enamels. Wedgwood used this decorating method on a number of other Stoneware ceramics including Black Basalt.

Different versions of the Cambridge Ale jug were made, including graduated sizes, some decorated, some with pewter flip-top lids, and some with matching circular ceramic bases. A large number of these jugs were made for Woollard & Hattersly of Cambridge for further sale to various colleges and universities. Some of the jugs were enameled with elaborate coats of arms representing the colleges and universities who purchased them. Wedgwood did produce Black Basalt Cambridge Ale jugs in the late 1880s with similar decorations, to those seen in the Black Basalt wares. Creamware was also used in the Cambridge Ale jugs shape, some accented with hand-painted decorations.

Dry-Body Stoneware: Cane Ware

Cane Ware, another local Staffordshire Stoneware, is characterized by its light buff color, made from a local Staffordshire sienna-colored clay called K-Marl. These wares often saw hard use in English kitchens for baking, food preparation, and as serving wares. The earliest Cane, introduced in 1770, was coarse and speckled with colors ranging from buff to almost brown. These early trials were rough, unrefined, and susceptible to burning and discoloration during the firing process.

By 1783, Wedgwood had further refined and improved his Cane formula. He achieved a consistent straw-like color and made the wares lighter in weight, yet stronger and more durable. Silica (sand) was added to the formula to make it more heat resistant. In addition, their color worked well with the fashion of the day, complimenting the neoclassical period aesthetics, which relied heavily on yellows for home decor.

Wedgwood's Cane included both a smooth body for tea and dinnerware and a coarse body for cooking and serving needs. The versatile Cane went on to become an important ornamental body in addition to its useful ware applications. This is seen by Cane's success with Bamboo Ware designs and encaustic painted decorative items. The coarse Cane body was hard and acid resistant, making it suitable for a wide variety of items such as for the garden, scientific equipment, and even baking and serving as with the game pie and pastry ware dishes.

Teapot, c. 1815. Cane Ware with smear-glaze, spaniel finial. *Courtesy of the Horn and Hoffman Collection.* $400-500.

Bamboo Ware

Chinese porcelain wine pots and vases popular in the early eighteenth century inspired Bamboo Ware, a Cane design first introduced in 1770. Bamboo Ware imitated short lengths of bamboo that were formed into teapots, root pots, bough pots, vases, and other shapes. These Bamboo designs were often decorated with encaustic or glossy enamels. Similar shapes existed in Basalt and later in Drab Ware. The name Bamboo Ware achieved such name recognition in the marketplace that catalogs briefly used the term to describe and garner interest in all Cane Ware.

In later years, Wedgwood produced similar Bamboo shapes in primrose colored Jasper with terracotta colored relief as well as a few examples in blue and white colored Jasper, which echoed the earlier cane designs. Wedgwood once again revived these classic bamboo shapes in the late 1990s, in a new line of their new Cane-colored Jasper, reviving the splendor of the old Cane Ware.

Encaustic Painting

Early successes of encaustic painting prompted Wedgwood to look for another ceramic upon which to expand this same decorative method. Having proved its versatility on Black Basalt, encaustic painting next appeared on Cane Ware during the period of 1770-1800. Wedgwood centered briefly on Jasper, but thinking that the chemical composition of Jasper might not be compatible, he directed his attentions to the Cane instead. Cane proved to be well suited to encaustic design, particularly on the Bamboo Ware shapes since it highlighted the curves and details.

In 1775, Thomas Bentley wrote to Josiah Wedgwood to inform him that encaustic painting on Jasper was indeed feasible. By this time however, encaustic decorated Cane had already succeeded, thus encaustic decorated Jasper was not pursued. It has been suggested that there could have been economical reasons behind the decision not to pursue encaustic painted Jasper. The Cane was made from less expensive local clays whereas the Jasper required more expensive imported ingredients — economics made Cane Ware the better choice. Jasper meanwhile was already making a name for itself in other artistic directions.

Game-Pie and Pastry Ware

From 1795-1805 England experienced a time of economic distress due to the Napoleonic Wars. Destroyed crops, flour shortages, and tightening economic conditions prompted a more conservative way of life. Grand dinners and tables full of lavishly decorated edibles gave way to simple, many times flourless foods. From this spawned the introduction of the game pie and pastry ware dishes — shapes of a decorative, yet useful nature.

The game pie dishes were food dishes with removable covers and inserts called "middles." Game pies were made primarily of ornate Cane Ware, with some made of majolica as well. Their purpose was to emulate the fine dining experience that had suffered in this period of economic crisis. Some of these items were purely ornamental; others were designed to hold more modest meals of rice and stewed meats replacing the scarce game the shapes emulated. These were often topped with finials in the shape of a vegetable or game animal to mimic their lost lavish lifestyle.

The main production period for pastry-ware, sometimes called piecrust ware, was between 1795-1805 during the Napoleonic Wars. As mentioned, this was a time of flour shortages and economic upheaval, so ingredients for piecrusts were scarce. These pastry-ware pieces included pies and other desert shapes, made to look like rich and elaborate desserts. Some were decorated with latticework to simulate the top of pastries and piecrusts. The dishes were filled with pie-fillings or custards. Wedgwood also produced imitation iced cakes in blue and white Jasper, which adorned dinner tables.

The Cane Ware game and pastry bodies could handle the heat of cooking and rigors of serving. Ornamentation consisted mainly of leaf, vine, vegetable, and game shapes, topped with finials of vegetable or animal shapes. Game pie dishes continued in production up to 1901. These items served a purpose in a time of hardship, but would later be revived as and reintroduced as decorative pieces years later.

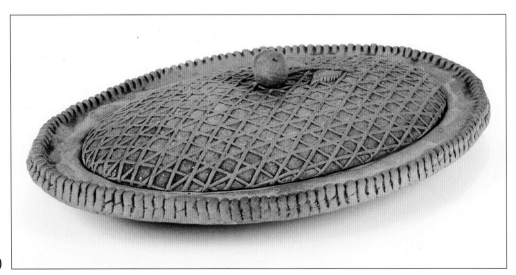

Pie dish, c. 1810. Pastry Ware, cherry finial and lattice raised pattern, 9". *Courtesy of the Chellis and Adams Collection.* $500-700.

Other Decoration Styles

Smear-glaze appeared on some Cane Ware pieces in 1815 as additional decoration. However, Cane belongs to the Stoneware family, which only needed glazing to prevent stains, so glazing was deemed unnecessary and was discontinued. Glazed items are therefore rarer and command higher prices than their later versions. After 1850, glazing on Cane returned briefly for use on game pie dish liners, know as "pie middles." Today, the more prized collectable game-pie dishes include intact middles.

Enameled decoration appeared on Cane from 1770-1800, typically in the form of hand-painted floral designs. Growing popularity led Wedgwood to produce great amounts of these wares during 1782-1800. Jasper applied relief was also used on some Cane Ware. They applied contrasting colors such as blue, against a yellow background, for a similar decorative effect as on the Jasper. Shapes were usually very similar if not outright borrowed from floral relief designs on the Jasper wares of the time. Wedgwood is well known to historians for having reused molds repeatedly on different ceramic bodies. This saved manufacturing costs and they could reuse shapes that had proven popular with consumers. It is very likely that the molds used for the Cane applied relief were created from Jasper Ware molds.

Dry-Body Stoneware: Drab Ware

Drab Ware is a dark olive-colored Stoneware that has enjoyed a modest level of popularity since its introduction in 1800. It was not produced in mass quantities and is generally thought of today as a more eclectic collectible. Drab was a product said to be typical of the Josiah Wedgwood II's period in that the shapes used in this ceramic, such as the Gothic and Celtic themed wares, had never been seen before in other ware. From about 1815 onward, Josiah Wedgwood II is responsible for taking the company from a classical style to a new, more creative neo-classical direction.

Drab Earthenware

The Drab can sometimes confuse collectors as it was produced in two different forms: Stoneware and as glazed earthenware. Drab tableware was introduced in 1820 as a stained earthenware. The color was closer to a brown than to the olive of the Drab Stoneware. The look and feel closely resembles the Creamware of the time and shared similar chemical composition. Drab can be referred to as a type of stained Creamware, often referred to as Drab Queen's Ware. The earliest examples are closer to brown in color, with the same delicate lightweight feel as early Creamware.

Drab Wares of the twentieth century have a lighter shade and are more decorative in shape than the early tableware. Drab tableware ceased sometime in the 1860s due to a movement toward whiter tableware, but was revived briefly in the twentieth century for some memorabilia type pieces. One such example included in this chapter is a pair of Dolphin-shaped candlesticks, a revival of a classical nineteenth century shape.

Drab Stoneware

Despite its rather bland appearance, the Drab encompassed the same artisanship as its Jasper and Cane counterparts. Drab often shared similar body-shapes and applied relief designs as can be seen in an accompanying photo with a Cane and Drab teapot of the same shape, shown side by side, but with different decoration. This further illustrates Wedgwood's practice of reusing shapes in different ceramic bodies. Wedgwood's Drab was a derivative of an older form that Staffordshire potters produced as a salt-glazed drab-colored ware since about 1720.

Relief decoration on Drab Ware evolved from new inspirations as well as from existing Jasper relief molds. Relief colors were primarily blue, lilac, and white. Some of the best pieces include applied relief in white and lilac for a contrasting effect on the Drab background. Glaze was unnecessary, but was sometimes used on the Drab Stoneware. Before the introduction of Wedgwood's Drab Ware, back in 1720, other potters had applied salt-glaze to their Drab Ware and smear-glaze was used on some Drab from about 1819 as additional adornment. Wedgwood's Drab did not need glazing to protect it from the rigors of day-to-day use.

Vase (no cover), c. 1800-1820. Drab Ware, white and lilac Acanthus leaves relief, 3.5" (mustache marks). *Author's Collection.* $400-450.

Gothic Revival

A Gothic revival emerged in the 1820s, triggered by changes in architectural trends. Their influence crossed over various other art forms, particularly those involved with home décor, including pottery. These events influencing this revival included Horace Walpole's villa at Strawberry Hill in the late eighteenth century. Strawberry Hill is said to be the first and most important architectural drive behind the Gothic Revival.

The Gothic revival trickled down to the pottery industry with the construction of the Fonthill Abbey, commissioned by William Bedford, based on the design of Salisbury Cathedral. William Bedford was an eccentric Gothic novelist of the time. These grand Gothic architectural images stirred the Gothic trend across England.

Teapot, c. 1820. White Stoneware with blue Arabesque relief, smear-glazing and Royal Crown finial. *Courtesy of the Slavid Collection.* $400-500.

Wedgwood's Drab Ware worked well with the Gothic themes. Shapes and designs were architectural influences including angular shapes, pointed arches on jugs, teapots, coffee pots, bowls, and wine coolers. These same Wedgwood Gothic shapes also appeared in Cane Ware and White Stoneware. Architecture has influenced Wedgwood designs at various times. In 1863, Celtic style and decoration emerged in the Drab body. These included intricate vases with raised and acid gold and white enamel decorations.

Dry-Body Stoneware: White Stoneware

The Stoneware body in Wedgwood's history that has received the least recognition is White Stoneware. This is mainly due to White Stoneware, "White," serving as the base or ground that was covered with a number of different glazing and painting styles. White is also not a commonly recognized ceramic body, as it did not appear very often in Wedgwood catalogs and marketing materials. It did not help White that it was frequently mislabeled as White Jasper. Nevertheless, the White did exist as Wedgwood Stoneware, making a few notable contributions to the company.

Due to its soft, highly porous surface, White Stoneware can almost always be found with either smear-glazes or salt-glazes. There has always been some confusion between the two glazing styles and how to properly identify them. The salt-glaze was a product of lining the kilns with salt, which would then adhere to the ceramic surface during firing. Conversely, the smear-glaze was ap-

plied with a brush. In some instances, close examination of a smear-glazed item will reveal the slightest hint of brush strokes in the glaze itself, a dead give-away. One could also consider that salt-glaze was not in regular production on Wedgwood, and certainly not beyond the 1700s. Furthermore, the salt-glaze leaves a slightly pitted surface, almost like the surface of an orange, whereas the smear-glaze is smoother.

Dry-Body Stoneware: Terracotta

In the history of Wedgwood, Terracotta is a term that has been misused and causes a great deal of confusion. Outside of the Wedgwood world, terracotta refers to orange-red colored Stoneware, but Wedgwood never produced any such wares. Early on in Wedgwood history, they did produce white terracotta, examples of which are scarce. At the time, the term "terra cotta" meant "dried earth" and thus could have been used to describe any earthenware pottery. In terms of what we know today as the orange-red bodied terra cotta, the closest Wedgwood product is the Terracotta-colored Jasper. The earliest Wedgwood Red Ware, was of course red, and the Rosso Antico, which replaced Red Ware, was somewhere in between the Red and the Terracotta Jasper from a color standpoint.

Further complicating the task of identifying Wedgwood, one must consider that the ceramic market has always been a highly competitive environment, as illustrated by the number of Wedgwood contemporaries and the number of imitators. Josiah Wedgwood learned early on to monitor the styles and trends of the day, once commenting that he could not afford to be out of fashion. With this in mind, Josiah Wedgwood was nearly as accomplished in marketing as he was in potting. Early Wedgwood advertisements indicate that Wedgwood often used the jargon of the day to describe his wares. If porcelain was the buzzword, he called his work porcelain. If the public was focused on china, Wedgwood had his China Ware. On the surface, this seems like good marketing, but it can tend to confuse historians and collectors. The term Terra Cotta is one name that may have been applied liberally to a variety of different ceramic bodies at one time or another.

Covered sugar pot, c. early 1800s. Rosso Antico with enameled Famille Rose style decorations. *Courtesy of the Chellis and Adams Collection.* $450-550.

Demitasse Cup & Saucer, 1805, Rosso Antico with Basalt Egyptian-style relief. Mark: "WEDGWOOD." *Courtesy of the Chellis and Adams Collection.* $600-650.

Pair of vases, c. early 1800s. Rosso Antico with black Egyptian decorations, 4". *Courtesy of the Slavid Collection.* $1,500-1,800.

Teapot, c. early 1800s. Rosso Antico with enameled Famille Rose style decorations. *Courtesy of the Chellis and Adams Collection.* $500-650.

Jug, c. early 1800s. Rosso Antico. *Courtesy of the Chellis and Adams Collection.* $350-450.

Teapot, c. 1810-1815. Rosso Antico in a parapet shape with applied white Chinese or Prunus flowers, flat cover, 4.5" x 9". *Courtesy of the Dorothy Lee-Jones Collection.* $1,000-1,300.

Large Cambridge Ale Jug, c. 1860. Rosso Antico, with coat of arms in enamel. *Courtesy of the Frazier Collection.* $75-150.

Teapot, c. 1840. Rosso Antico with silver mounts, and silver rosebud knob. *Courtesy of the Slavid Collection.* $700-800.

Reclining infant figure a.k.a. "sleeping boy", c. 1800s. Rosso Antico, in the style of Duquesnoy. This figure was one of *Five Boys of Fiammingo. Courtesy of the Slavid Collection.* $1,000-1,500.

Teapot, c. late 1700s. Cane Ware, oval-shape with bamboo styled body and lion finial. *Courtesy of the Chellis and Adams Collection.* $400-500.

Honey pot, c. late 1700s. Smear-glazed Cane Ware in beehive shape, (Wedgwood mark). *Courtesy of the Chellis and Adams Collection.* $450-550.

Pitcher, c. 1895-1900. Kenlock Ware in Rosso Antico with enameled coat of arms of Nova Scotia, printed: "Kenlock Ware" on bottom, 9.25". *Courtesy of the Frazier Collection.* $75-100.

196

Teapot, c. late 1700s. Oval-shape, Cane Ware with glazed basket weave body design. *Courtesy of the Chellis and Adams Collection.* $400-450.

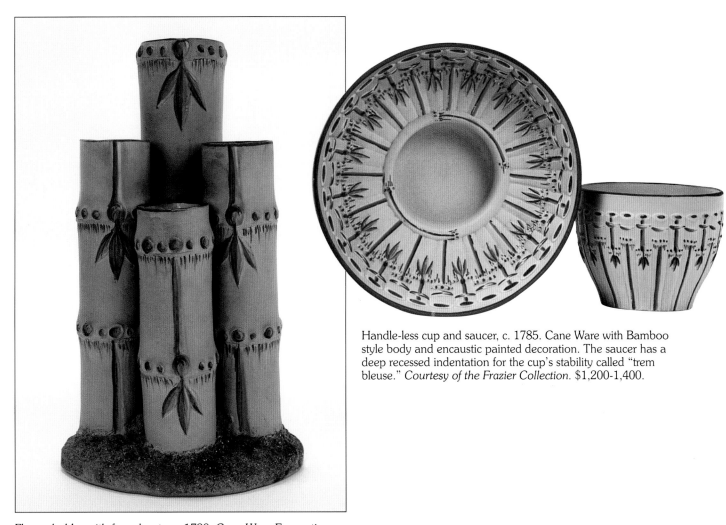

Handle-less cup and saucer, c. 1785. Cane Ware with Bamboo style body and encaustic painted decoration. The saucer has a deep recessed indentation for the cup's stability called "trem bleuse." *Courtesy of the Frazier Collection.* $1,200-1,400.

Flower holder with four shoots, c. 1790. Cane Ware Encaustic-painted. *Courtesy of the Goldman Collection.* $5,000-7,000.

Cane, mini-creamer in Bamboo-ware styled, c. 1790. *Courtesy of the Slavid Collection.* $400.

Creamer, c. early 1800s. Smear glazed Cane Ware with blue relief. *Courtesy of the Chellis and Adams Collection.* $300-400.

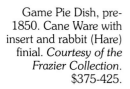

Game Pie Dish, pre-1850. Cane Ware with insert and rabbit (Hare) finial. *Courtesy of the Frazier Collection.* $375-425.

198

Custard Cup, c. 1700s. Smear-glazed Cane Ware with white Acanthus leaf relief, 3". *Author's Collection.* $110-130.

Teapot with braided handle, c. early 1800s. Drab Ware, glazed with Gothic designs. *Courtesy of the Chellis and Adams Collection.* $600-675.

199

Teapot, 1790-1810. Smear-glazed Stoneware, marks: impressed "WEDGWOOD." *Courtesy of the Frazier Collection.* $850-900.

Coffee Biggin (a.k.a. tea infuser), c. 1800s. Smear glazed Drab Ware with white applied relief of wreaths of aster rose, berry, and pomegranate. This set is complete with all five pieces. The Biggin was invented in 1803 and was produced in Queen's Ware as well as in dry-bodied stoneware, 4.25" x 6". *Courtesy of the Dorothy Lee-Jones Collection.* $1,600-2,200.

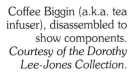

Coffee Biggin (a.k.a. tea infuser), disassembled to show components. *Courtesy of the Dorothy Lee-Jones Collection.*

Drab Ware teapot with blue relief, octagonal shape, c. 1830. $200-400. Cane Ware teapot, octagonal shape, c. 1820s. *Courtesy of the Horn and Hoffman Collection.* $200-400.

Plate, December 1868. Drab Queen's Ware, no other design, (DIW mark), 7.5". *Author's Collection.* $80-120.

Honey pot, 1999. Drab Queen's Ware in the shape of a beehive. *Courtesy of the Frazier Collection.* $50-80.

Pair of dolphin shaped candleholders, c. 1999. Drab Ware (Earthenware), glazed, 10 7/8". *Courtesy of the Frazier Collection.* $50-65.

Sprigging mold, c. 1800. White unglazed Stoneware mold of *Sacrifice to Cupid. Courtesy of the Frazier Collection.* $100-150.

Sprigging mold, c. 1800. White unglazed Stoneware mold of *Flora. Courtesy of the Frazier Collection.* $100-150.

Sprigging mold, c. late 1700s. Stoneware, floral relief, 2.5". *Author's Collection*. $110-120.

Mortar & pestle, c. 1800. *Courtesy of the Frazier Collection*. $150-200.

Teapot, c. 1820. White Stoneware, gothic shaped, with
smear-glazing. *Courtesy of the Slavid Collection.* $350-450.

Vase without cover, c. 1860-1862. Lilac, green on
white stoneware, acanthus leaves and bell flower
designs. *Courtesy of the Slavid Collection.* $400.

Pair of Bough pots with pierced lids and candleholder, c. 1785.
White terracotta Stoneware with Pearl glaze. Decorated with swag
and bows, rouletted top border and curved vertical flutes on body.
Courtesy of the Dorothy Lee-Jones Collection. $800-1,000.

Wedgwood trial piece, c. 1880. Solid green
tinted Stoneware with gold gilt, 6". *Courtesy
of the Slavid Collection.* $650-700.

Chapter 8
Bone China

In the early 1800s, a trend emerged among the English and American markets for whiter, more refined wares than the popular Creamware. English potters tried to satisfy this need by mimicking Chinese porcelain by combining ingredients such as China Clay and China Stone, but found it difficult and expensive to reproduce. China Clay and China Stone, used in porcelain, were both readily available in England. China Clay was the whitest of clays and the China Stone when fired at extremely high temperatures turn into a hard, glass-like solid surface. Together they formed porcelain.

Importing Chinese porcelain was another option to satisfy the demand; however, it was expensive to transport, meaning only the wealthy could afford the high prices. English potters would continue their experimentation and would develop Bone China, a porcelain derivative, with which to compete in the porcelain market.

Bone China is similar to porcelain in whiteness and lightness of weight, since it uses both China Clay and China Stone. The key ingredient that differentiates the Bone China is animal bone or bone ash (calcium phosphate). The animal bone has a lower melting point than that of the China Stone, so when they are mixed together the bone lowers the combined firing temperature needed to produce Bone China. A lower firing temperature required less fuel, thus decreasing the overall cost of the piece.

First Period Bone China

Wedgwood began producing Bone China in 1812 as tea wares (sets) to compete with the popular Chinese porcelain tea wares. Other Staffordshire potters had already been producing Bone China, seizing on the public's demand for porcelain. The Wedgwood company was late capitalizing on this trend since it was heavily focused on Creamware production and had lost much of its innovation and forward thinking with the passing of Josiah Wedgwood in 1795.

Vase, 1885. Golconda Ware, developed by George Marsden, with flora embossed design. *Courtesy of the Frazier Collection.* $600-800.

Wedgwood artists such as John Cutts decorated Bone China with painted landscapes, birds, flowers, and printed enamel patterns with an Oriental influenced style. The public poorly received these styles as they were favoring styles of the Regency Period (1805-1873). The name for the Regency Period came from the Prince Regent who became King George IV in 1810 since his father, George III, had become mentally incapacitated. The English Bone China of this time came to represent flamboyant taste with bold decorative features and heavily gilded decoration. This was a transitioning point when the common man was able to enjoy the opulence of the aristocracy through more sophisticated ceramics, previously too expensive for commoners. The less expensive Bone China put the average folk on par with the wealthy. The work of John Cutts was of good quality, but stylistically it was the wrong look for the time.

In Wolf Mankowitz's book, *Wedgwood*, he suggests that part of Bone China's failure was attributed to the marketing inexperience of Josiah Wedgwood II. In retrospect, his father was the driving force for marketing, trend development, and innovation for the company. Josiah Wedgwood believed in spending time preparing the market and fueling the anticipation of his clients long before the release of a new product. When Josiah Wedgwood II released Bone China, it was rushed to market and lacked the decorative link to the themes and styles of the day. Wedgwood considered these pieces a failure and ended their production in 1822.

The markings from this period were troublesome, which further illustrated Wedgwood's difficulties with Bone China. Wedgwood marked these first period wares with red printed "WEDGWOOD" all in capitals with serifs. This mark was printed over the glaze before firing the piece again at a lower temperature. This led to the marks rubbing off the pieces during regular use. In order to make the mark more permanent, Wedgwood began applying blue marks under the glaze while they were in the process of decorating the piece. Impressed marks never appeared on Bone China during the first period.

Second Period Bone China

Wedgwood enhanced its Bone China decorative designs and themes, and in 1878 initiated their Second

Cup and saucer, c. 1815. First period Bone China with scrolled yellow and polychrome "Mandarin" pattern, Chinese figures in irregular framed cartouches, on a yellow and white ground. *Courtesy of the Slavid Collection.* $250-350.

Period of Bone China production. This Second Period Bone China was lighter in weight, distinctly whiter in color, and was decorated with strong, Japanese-influenced flora patterns. This time the market welcomed Wedgwood's Bone China and its new, improved look. Due to Second Period Bone China's success, Wedgwood expanded its product line to include full dinner services.

Printed marks became a more regular practice in 1878 across all Wedgwood wares. The first marks used on Second Period Bone China included an outline of Wedgwood's Portland Vase with the "Wedgwood" name below. Decades later, the Portland Vase would become an official part of the company's corporate logo.

Over the years, Wedgwood continued to improve its marking processes and in 1900 began using smaller and more sharply defined images of the Portland Vase and "Wedgwood" stamp. Impressed "Wedgwood" marks were rare on Second Period Bone China as the firing process tended to fire out the impression, rendering it unreadable. In 1937, Wedgwood would add the words "Bone China" to the markings.

Alpine Pink Bone China

Alpine Pink is a stained form of Bone China, made by adding coloring oxides to the mix. Wedgwood's Norman Wilson developed Alpine Pink in 1936 for tableware shapes and nautilus shell shaped wares. Wedgwood conducted a number of experiments with other stains on Bone China, produced in small quantities. These included shades of celadon, blue, yellow, and lilac, identified by the name of the color shown along with the other markings on the bottom of each piece. Alpine Pink was also used as the base in producing a series of enamel-painted figures such as the John Jorrocks and Ballet Dancers figures.

Golconda Ware

Golconda Ware describes a decorative design applied to a Bone China body. Golconda is easy to identify with its signature raised gold design, similar to that of Auro Basalt (refer to Chapter Four). A distinguishing feature of Golconda is the gold paste used to create the raised leaf-like designs that typically adorn the pieces. Enamel is also occasionally an accent to the gold. While the gold design is raised and very prominent, it is not as thick as an applied relief such as those seen on Jasper pieces. Golconda was the creation of George Marsden and was only produced in a limited quantity around 1885.

Powder Blue Bone China

Powder Blue is a decoration applied on top of a Bone China ground, developed by James Hodjkiss and George Adams of Wedgwood. Wedgwood introduced Powder Blue Bone China in 1912, though other potters such as Copeland had been producing similar, lesser quality forms since 1910. The design was based on a Chinese method of textured coloring on porcelain, called "bleu suffle." Bleu suffle involved a variety of steps. The surface is prepared with oil and then Chinese potters applied a cobalt blue powder to the porcelain using a length of bamboo covered at one end with a silk-screen. After firing the piece, the surface hardened with a slight textured feel to it from the silk-screening process. The motivation behind Wedgwood pursuing this new decoration came from a suggestion by A.M. Powell of J. Powell & Sons, a ceramics retailer and relative of Wedgwood artist Alfred Powell.

Wedgwood's Powder Blue started with a single applied blue ground on their Bone China. Unlike the attempts of Wedgwood's competitors as well as the Chinese potters' bleu suffle method, Wedgwood used a blue over-glaze. This helped control the quality of the finish during firing. Wedgwood also textured the wet surface with a fine sponge to simulate the surface texture of the silk-screen method and placed a fine layer of silk-gauze on the blue, which was removed, leaving behind a slight texture. Wedgwood's Powder Blue wares were sometimes highlighted with gold in a diaper pattern and Oriental figures. A diaper pattern refers to an Oriental created pattern consisting of interlocking geometric figure that seem to go on to infinity.

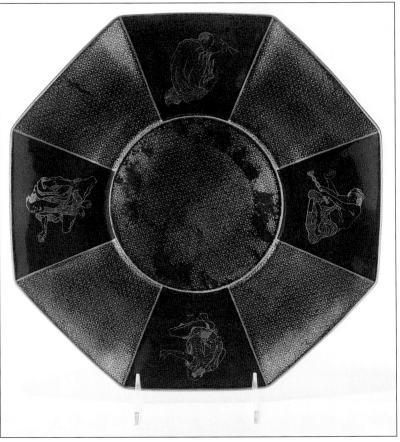

Octagon plate, c. early 1900s. Powder blue ground and gold diaper patterned alternating panels and Japanese figures, pattern Z4604. Printed on the reverse with the Wedgwood Portland vase mark, "William H. Plummer & Co. New York." *Author's Collection*. $300-350.

Other Powder-type decorations were used in such colors as ruby and pink. These decorations, like the Powder Blue were often referred to as a form of Lustre as they were often augmented with Lustre decoration. Powder Blue could arguably be categorized in either the Lustre or Bone China categories. I categorize it as Bone China with Powder-type decorations, since most Wedgwood pieces are based on the ground or actual composition of the piece, rather than just the application.

Liberty Ware Service

The Liberty Service is an interesting and limited issue Bone China (and Queen's Ware) table service. Toward the end of World War I, Mrs. Robert Coleman Taylor of New York had the idea to produce a patriotic table service to raise money in support of the War Relief Fund. Taylor took orders by subscription and ran the business out of her home. Wedgwood produced these wares for a limited time between 1917-1918, in both Bone China and in Queen's Ware. Wedgwood shipped these wares to a New York ceramics retailer, William Plummer and Co. and Mrs. Taylor distributed them to supporters from her own home.

Mrs. H. Snowden Marshell created the design for the Liberty wares, which included the shield of America surrounded by flags of the various allied countries. The shield was a pointed shield shape in which the top portion was blue with white stars and had red and white stripes running vertically down from the blue. Copper plates were used to transfer the patterns to the plates.

In all, only 9,251 total pieces of Liberty Ware were produced, 4,985 in Bone China and another 4,266 in Queen's Ware. All orders that were taken prior to Armistice Day (the end of the war) were fulfilled, after which the pattern was permanently discontinued. The copper plates used to apply the designs were also destroyed. In 1924, a small book was published on the Liberty Ware service in which the subscribers were all listed. It mentions that $14,203 was raised for war relief and it outlined the distributions of the money raised.

Artist: Eduardo L. Paolozzi

In 1970, Wedgwood contracted freelance artist Eduardo Paolozzi, to design a limited edition set of six Bone China plates with very unusual decorative patterns. He called them *Variations on a Geometric Theme* and they consisted of circles, squares, and other shapes that were silk-screened on the plate in organized patterns. The colors differed on each, from red, orange to yellow, contrasted by black or gold to highlight the shapes and geometric designs. The example pictured in this chapter has an orange base, with purple and gold silk-screened designs of circles, squares, and lines. Wedgwood produced a limited number of 200 sets, making them quite rare. These plates are some of the most unusual and atypical Wedgwood Bone China pieces and can command hundreds of dollars per plate.

In 1987, Paolozzi designed another limited edition set of bone china plates called the *Kalkulium Suite*. These were white with colored geometric designs around the edges of the plates.

Stone China

In 1800, the potting firm of Turner developed a thick, coarser form of porcelain called Stone China. It was a dense and hard, porcelain-like ware composed of China stone, China clay, flint, blue clay, and blue stain. These pieces centered around Chinese patterns underglazed

Liberty Ware pieces from a tea service, 1917-1918, with enamel decoration and gilt trim. These were part of a tea ware and dinner wares set that were made, and sold, to benefit various allied war charities. *Courtesy of the Rosen Collection.* $200-300.

with blue printed designs or ornamental style prints with on-glaze enameling and gilding.

Stone China was thicker than Bone China and therefore not translucent. The look Turner was trying to achieve was Stoneware-like porcelain. Wedgwood produced its first experimental pieces in 1817 and continued refining and improving the ware until about 1822. Wedgwood discontinued its Stone China production in 1861.

Plate, c. 1817-1829. Stone China with colored enamel Lustre, Chinese garden with peonies, rock, bamboo, and standing heron facing right, 8 1/8". Reverse side includes underglaze print "WEDGWOOD STONE CHINA." *Courtesy of the Dorothy Lee-Jones Collection.* $150-200.

Bowl with two cups and saucers, c. 1815. Yellow, light green, and gold with vine/leaf texture and gold tendrils, 6.5". (Red Wedgwood mark). *Courtesy of the Chellis and Adams Collection.* $300-500.

Tea ware, c. 1815. First Period Bone China with vine/leaf texture and gold tendrils. Pattern no. 30, (red Wedgwood mark). *Courtesy of the Dorothy Lee-Jones Collection.* $300-500.

First Period Bone China Tea ware, enlarged to show detail.

210

Three pieces of First Period Bone China, c. 1815. Chinese or Japanese design. The saucer is of the tea-bowl style, in which the run-off from the tea would be consumed directly from the bowl/saucer. Back of plate reads "No. 570," (red Wedgwood mark). *Courtesy of the Chellis and Adams Collection.* $250-300.

Octagonal Plate, 1878-1880. Printed with Willow Pattern, enamel coloring of red, black, brown, and pale ochre, 8.875". Gilding is on the trunk, branches, and border. *Courtesy of the Dorothy Lee-Jones Collection.* $90-160.

Pair of octagonal-shaped cups and saucers, c. 1878-1891. Features blue painted Oriental designs and gold trim. (Portland Vase stamp with WEDGWOOD sans serif, both marks printed in blue). *Author's Collection.* Pair: $100-130.

Cup and saucer, c. 1923. Yellow and white design, gold laurels, red and blue flower border design. *Courtesy of the Frazier Collection.* $50-75.

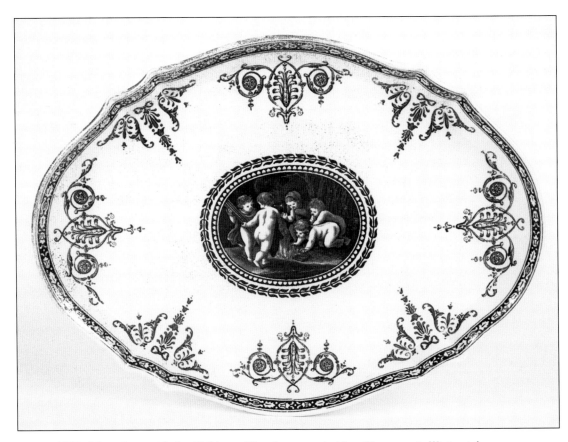

Tray, c. 1893. Silver-shape with the *Children of Bacchus* scene in blue. The scene is *Winter*, taken from Giovani Battista Cipriani's *Season* series. *Courtesy of the Frazier Collection.* $300-350.

Dinner plate, c. 1900s. Alpine Pink with floral print around the rim and gold gilding around the edges, pattern WH3704, 10.75". *Author's Collection.* $25-30.

Figurine of John Jorrocks, c. 1890s. In Alpine Pink, modeled by Montague A. Weaver-Bridgeman, with "John Jorrocks" printed on front of the base. John Jorrocks was a character from *New Sporting Magazine* in the 1930s, created by Robert Smith Satees. In addition to a series of plates with Satees' characters, Wedgwood also produced a Black Basalt version of this figurine. *Courtesy of the Slavid Collection.* $1,200.

Ballet Dancers figurine, c. 1932. In Alpine Pink, figurine by Kathleen Goodwin and painted in enamel by Arthur Dale Holland. *Courtesy of the Slavid Collection.* $1,200-1,300.

Cup and saucer, c. 1895. Blue transfer print, inside the cup lip reads, "WE'LL TAK A CVP O'KINDNESS YET FOR DAYS O'AULD LANGSYNE," Pattern #Y8430. *Courtesy of the Frazier Collection.* $75-100.

Plate, c. 1910. *Cupid* design in center after Batolozzi and grapevine border with gilt highlights, (X7067 mark), signed by artist Joseph P. Thorley, 8.75". *Courtesy of the Slavid Collection.* $275-300.

Vase with handles, Golconda Ware, by George Marsden, 1885. *Courtesy of the Chellis and Adams Collection.* $600-800.

Cup and saucer, c. 1903. From the Theodore Roosevelt Presidential
Service. *Courtesy of the Chellis and Adams Collection.* $400-600.

Cup and saucer, c. 1910. Powder Blue. *Courtesy of the Horn and Hoffman Collection.* $300-400.

Melba cup, c. 1910. Powder Blue with hand-painted
Chinese figure in an outdoor setting. *Courtesy of the
Horn and Hoffman Collection.* $300-500.

Powder Ruby Lustre vase, c. 1910, $300-500. Powder Blue cylindrical vase with dragon
motif designs in gold, similar to Dragon designs on Lustres, c. 1910, $300-500. Powder
blue Lustre bowl, c. 1910, $300-500. *Courtesy of the Horn and Hoffman Collection.*

Wine labels, c. 1926. "Burgundy" and "Sherry" leaf shapes, 1 7/8", with chain.
"Wedgwood England" corn mark, retailer "T. Goode & Co. LTD London."
Courtesy of the Slavid Collection. $275 each.

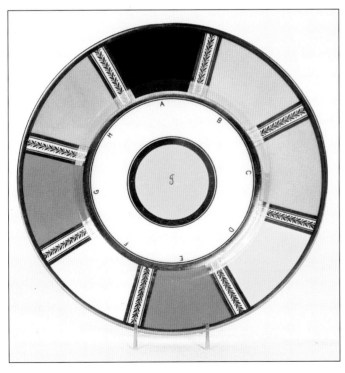

Sample plate, c. 1935. Showcases different types of monograms,
front has "W. M. H. Plummer" printed near the top. 10.5".
Courtesy of the Slavid Collection. $400.

Sample plate, c. 1900. Showcases different coloring
possibilities offered, "Laburnum Yellow" printed on back,
10.5". *Courtesy of the Slavid Collection*. $600.

Candlestick, c. late 1800s. Cut designs and enamel coloring with gilt highlights, 9.5". *Courtesy of the Slavid Collection*. $375.

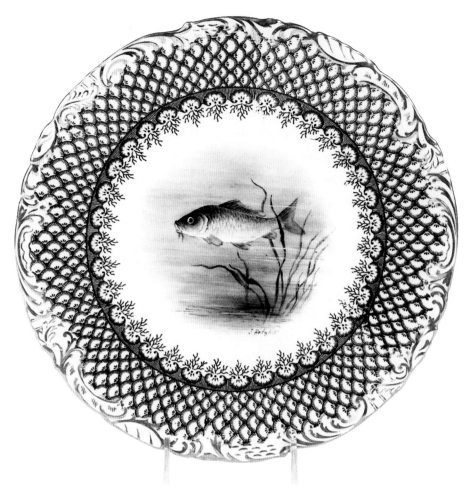

Carp plate, c. late 1800s. Gilt and enamel decoration, scale border signed by the artist J. Hodgkiss, 8.75". *Courtesy of the Slavid Collection*. $375.

Lithopane, c. 1920. White and blue, *Laurel Garland Dancing Hours* design. *Courtesy of the Slavid Collection*. $100-200.

Octagon shaped plate, c. 1927. Features the home of Edgar Allen Poe
by Isabel Marshall. *Courtesy of the Rosen Collection.* $55-70.

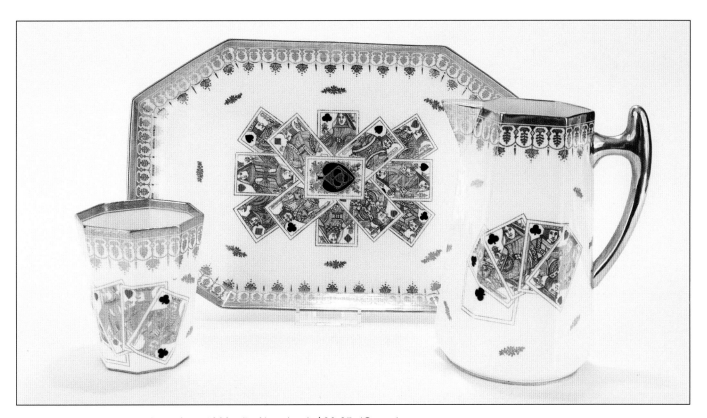

Tea wares with playing card motifs, c. 1900s. (Left) tankard, $30-35. (Center)
platter, $35-40. (Right) pitcher, $35-40. *Courtesy of the Rosen Collection.*

Plate, c. 1895-1900. In the Royal shape with enamel painted decoration, gilt highlights and parrot and flora motifs in hand-painted enamel. *Courtesy of the Slavid Collection.* $300.

Trumpet shaped vase, c. 1920. Cobalt blue ground and hand-painted panels designed by Joseph Thorely. *Courtesy of the Horn and Hoffman Collection.* $200-300.

Shell plate, c. 1850. Floral Bleeding Heart design. *Courtesy of the Frazier Collection.* $125-150.

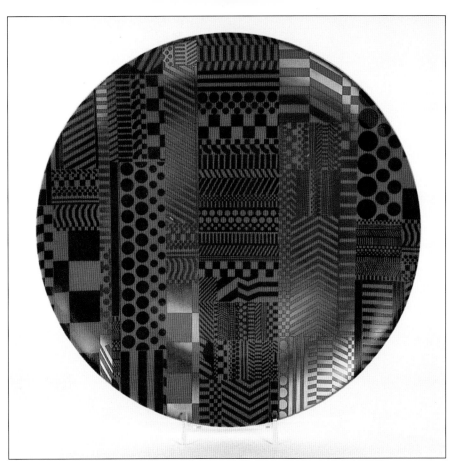

Sir Eduardo Paolozzi plate, c. 1971. Silk-screened designs *Variations on a Geometric Theme*, 10.5". *Courtesy of the Slavid Collection*. $250-300.

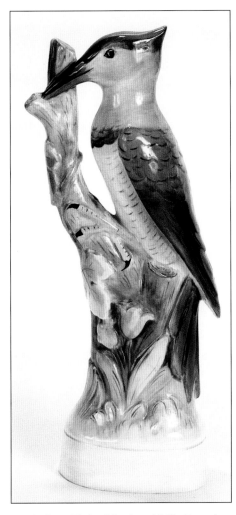

"Flicka" or "Flicker" bird, c. 1940. Part of a series of bird figures after the Audubon's *Birds of America* designed by Herbert W. Palliser, painted by Arthur Dale Holland, and commissioned by Wedgwood retailer, W. H. Plummer & Co. of New York. 9.25". *Courtesy of the Slavid Collection*. $950.

Lady Godiva plate, 1990. From the "Feats of Festivals" series of ten plates. This image depicts Lady Godiva on her famous ride, also shown is the image of Peeping Tom looking upon her. Signed by Jerry Rhodes. *Courtesy of the Frazier Collection*. $25-35.

Toucan, 1993. From the Noah's Ark Collection, 4.75". *Author's Collection.* $40-55.

Wedding cake topper, 1996. All white with a hint of color on bride's flowers. Gift from the Author to his wife for their wedding cake. Martin Evans design. *Author's Collection.* $90-100.

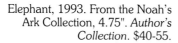

Elephant, 1993. From the Noah's Ark Collection, 4.75". *Author's Collection.* $40-55.

Bowl, c. 1974. The "100th run for the roses May 4, 1974, Kentucky Derby." Painted by Richard Stone Reeves who has painted nearly every great racehorse. The bowl features five Kentucky Derby champions on the bowl. Limited edition of 1,142. 9.5". *Courtesy of the Rosen Collection.* $400-500.

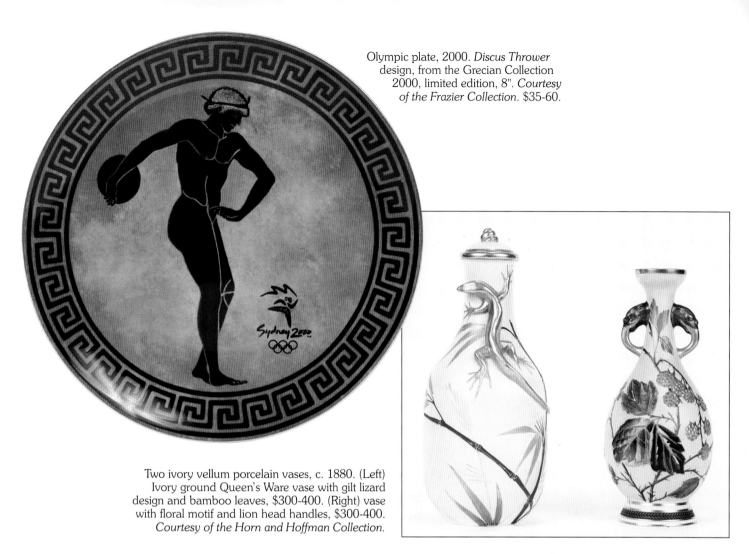

Olympic plate, 2000. *Discus Thrower* design, from the Grecian Collection 2000, limited edition, 8". *Courtesy of the Frazier Collection.* $35-60.

Two ivory vellum porcelain vases, c. 1880. (Left) Ivory ground Queen's Ware vase with gilt lizard design and bamboo leaves, $300-400. (Right) vase with floral motif and lion head handles, $300-400. *Courtesy of the Horn and Hoffman Collection.*

Three covered potpourri jars. (Left) Cream underbody with plum ground and enamel flowers, with raised gold leaf, pierced cover, c. 1885, $600-700. (Center) Bone China with Tofts Patent design, c. 1880s, $700-900. (Right) Golconda style decoration with pierced cover and inner lid, c. 1885, $600-700. *Courtesy of the Horn and Hoffman Collection.*

Porcelain vase, c. 1885. Ivory glaze with floral and bird designs, 14.5". *Courtesy of the Horn and Hoffman Collection.* $800-900.

Porcelain vase, c. 1885. Ivory glaze with floral and bird designs, 14.5". *Courtesy of the Frazier Collection.* $800-900.

Four-piece inkwell, c. mid-1800s. Porcelain, Wedgwood mark.
Courtesy of the Chellis and Adams Collection. $300-450.

Stone China platter, c. 1827-1861. Marked on reverse side with underglaze print:
"WEDGWOOD STONE CHINA." *Courtesy of the Slavid Collection.* $250-300.

Chapter 9
Lustre Ware and Lustre Decoration

In the late 1700s, Josiah Wedgwood experimented with the idea of lustre on Wedgwood wares. He had come across lustre in his search to make his Etruscan and Greek-themed Basalt vases look more similar to the bronzed art of the Classical Age. Lustre had been in existence long before Wedgwood's time and he wondered if it could be adapted to his Basalt wares. Though Wedgwood would experiment with various lustre techniques before his death in 1795, he unfortunately would not see the depth and breadth of lustre possibilities that the Wedgwood company would later explore.

The term lustre refers to a style of ceramic decoration based on the use of metal and metal oxides which created metallic and iridescent effects on ceramics. Wedgwood incorporated lustre techniques into its wares since the early 1800s. Along the way, the company greatly expanded the uses of lustre decoration.

Octagon bowl, c. 1916. Fairyland Lustre. *Courtesy of the Chellis and Adams Collection.* $3,000-5,000.

Wedgwood produced many forms of lustre that fall into three categories: Iridescent Lustre, Metal Lustre, and Commercial Lustre. With Iridescent Lustre thin films of metal act like a glaze and typically coat the entire object. It may or may not look like metal, but the reflective, iridescent metallic properties are unmistakable. Metal or Metallized Lustre appears like the metal itself. Metal is applied in a specific pattern, not coating the entire piece but accenting specific areas or parts of the design. Commercial Lustre, also referred to as Liquid Lustre, is the most mass producible of the lustres, with a typically painted-on lustre finish.

Pink, Purple, and Moonlight Lustre

In 1805, Wedgwood introduced iridescent Pink Lustre under the direction of Josiah Wedgwood II. Pink Lustre was a reflective, pink metallic film on top of a glazed piece. This effect was created by painting a mixture of gold and oil onto the piece. The piece was then fired in a reduction kiln, a kiln that is charged with carbon monoxide rather than oxygen. This carbon monoxide atmosphere in the kiln caused the gold to experience a chemical reaction that turned the gold into a shade of pink or purple.

A popular variation of the Pink Lustre was a mottled form that is popularly called Moonlight Lustre, now properly termed Variegated Lustre. Moonlight was created by splashing the piece with gold and platinum mixtures. Typically, a feather was used to create the mottled and variegated appearance. The level of gold concentration determined the depth of color; more gold resulted in a deeper shade. Shapes included goblets, potpourri vases, and pastille burners. Wedgwood also used Moonlight Lustre for a new line of shell and nautilus shaped wares that included simple plates, wall pockets, and serving dishes. Moonlight Lustre's popularity quickly spread and soon competing potters were heavily copying Wedgwood's Moonlight Lustre.

Mug, c. 1910. Pink Lustre decorated by Alfred Powell, 3". "Wedgwood England" Portland vase mark, "1340." *Courtesy of the Slavid Collection.* $600.

Silver Resist Lustre

Silver Resist Lustre is a form of Metallized Lustre in which metallic decorative patterns are incorporated into the design. The resist in its name refers to a method of controlling the lustre's placement, restricting it to a specific area or pattern on the piece. This requires the piece to be prepared with a special coating of a removable mixture such as sugar (or honey) and glycerin. This prevents the metal from adhering to unwanted areas of the piece during firing. The mixture is later rubbed off the piece, taking with it any metal not meant to be part of the finished pattern.

Creamer, c. 1950s. Creamware body, silver resist with gothic arch designs, augmented with Lustre decoration and hand-painted red enamel highlights, pattern CM52255. *Author's Collection.* $70-85.

In actuality, Silver Resist Lustre uses no silver in the process. Due the rapid rate at which silver tarnishes, Wedgwood substituted a slower to tarnish metal — platinum. After coating the piece with a clear glossy glaze, the platinum resembled silver.

Rhodian Ware

Rhodian Ware is a colorful free-hand enamel painting style, characterized by Islamic influenced flora patterns and Silver Resist Lustre highlights. Wedgwood artists who used the free-hand style included Alfred and Louise Powell and Millicent Taplin. Rhodian Ware did not generate widespread interest in the market. Wedgwood only produced limited quantities of these wares between 1920 and 1930. A similar, Persian-styled Rhodian Ware was also produce in the 1890s and again in the 1920s, concurrent to the Islamic period.

Artists: Alfred and Louise Powell

The work of Alfred H. Powell and Louise Powell began in a collective sense in the early 1900s. This was the time of the Arts and Crafts Movement, which began in England and extended internationally. It was a migration back to the basics: simplistic designs and pure artisanship, a step away from industrially and mass-produced wares. The theme in the pottery industry at the time was to put a human touch back into art. This was not a new idea to Wedgwood, as its previous experiences with individual artists were very successful.

In 1906, Alfred H. Powell married Ada Louise Lessore, granddaughter of Wedgwood artist Emile Lessore. Alfred and Louise went on to produce numerous hand-painted works of art and helped rejuvenate hand painting. They worked together in a studio that Wedgwood setup for them, where they collaborated on numerous creations. It has been said that their technique and style were almost indistinguishable from one another, so much so that their designs were often accredited simply as those of "Alfred H. and Louise Powell."

The designs painted by Alfred and Louise Powell fell into two categories: those of simple floral designs on tableware and those of a decorative nature, similar to the Islamic-influenced Rhodian Ware. In addition, the Powells would often purchase from Wedgwood undecorated Queen's Ware blanks, upon which they would paint custom scenes of homes or historical buildings to order as commissioned by their customers. The Queen's Ware blanks, once decorated, were returned to Wedgwood's Etruria factory for firing.

Their success generated great interest at Wedgwood. This led Wedgwood to seek other talented ceramic artists, who would be trained and supervised by Wedgwood's Millicent Taplin. The Powells discontinued their working

Creamer, c. 1913. Copper Lustre, decorated by Louise Powell. *Courtesy of the Frazier Collection.* $55-85.

relationship with Wedgwood in 1930, but continued to paint for several more years using Wedgwood blanks when commissioned by their customers.

Artist: Millicent J. Taplin

In 1917, Wedgwood hired Millicent J. Taplin, a part-time student at the Stoke and Burslem Schools of Art. Her early work focused on Rhodian Wares under Alfred Powell's tutelage. As her experience grew, she worked developing some of her own patterns, incorporating hand-painted flora designs augmented with Silver Lustre highlighting. During World War II when a number of the employees went off to serve and the need for decorative wares dropped off, Taplin took up full-time teaching at the Stoke School of Art. After the war, Taplin returned to Wedgwood and headed up the hand-painted China and earthenware departments until her retirement in 1962.

Commercial Lustre Ware

Just after the Victorian Majolica trend ended around 1910 and just before the Modernistic Art Deco movement of the 1930s, Wedgwood pursued an Oriental-influenced direction, as was the trend in the market at the time. Wedgwood utilized Liquid Lustres to create iridescent metallic sheens over intricately detailed Oriental and Fantasy motifs. These pieces would be characterized by their surface finishes, which reacted to light, creating a metallic glint.

Bowl, c. 1928. Copper Lustre with polychrome and enamel decoration by Millicent Taplin, 8.5". *Courtesy of the Horn and Hoffman Collection.* $400-450.

In the 1920s, under the direction of designer S. M. Daisy Makeig-Jones, Wedgwood developed a style of ceramics focused entirely around this new lustre called Commercial Ware Lustre. This represented a bold new direction for Wedgwood. Though Lustre Wares were not new to Wedgwood, the artistry of Daisy Makeig-Jones pioneered the company into a radically different direction. This new Lustre Ware prospered until it was forced out of production by the economic hardships of World War II. Today, Lustre Ware collectables are very expensive and heavily sought after, driven by lack of supply due to their short production period, as well as the high quality of artisanship and unique designs.

Commercial Lustre was a brush-on type of decoration sometimes referred to as a Liquid Lustre. The Lustre, in liquid form, was painted on with a delicate brush. Then the piece was fired in a low-temperature Lustre kiln to harden the surface coating. This was a complicated and tenuous process, as a less-than-perfect application would render the finished piece useless. Too little applied Lustre would burn off and not create the iridescence effect at all; too much would lead to flaking and cracking. The kiln temperature was also critical, as too much heat damaged and dissipated the iridescent effect.

The process was completed with gold, commonly used on these Lustre Wares to highlight the designs of the piece. The gold had to be ground into a powder and mixed with mercury, dried, then applied to the designs and patterns already marked out on the piece. The gold was applied to the designs on the piece, which were sticky from the applied print. Any excess was then brushed off. The edges were hand-painted and then the piece was fired again in a lower-temperature kiln.

Commercial Lustres fall into three distinct categories, Ordinary Lustre, Fairyland Lustre, and a miscellaneous category that includes Celtic and Persian designs augmented with metallic decoration. Each of these were designed by and produced under the direction of Daisy Makeig-Jones.

Commercial Lustre: Ordinary Lustre

Ordinary Lustres (a.k.a. China Lustre) incorporated patterns of painted animal and insect designs on top of colored staining and mottling. Often these Ordinary Lustres are referred to as Fairyland, but they are different. Ordinary Lustre, similar to the Fairyland, incorporated complimentary color combinations inside and outside of each piece. One color of lustre would coat the outside of the object and a different color coated the inside. These included luxurious colors not before seen on Wedgwood such as mother-of-pearl, ruby, and orange — all in a streak-like, mottled patterns. The color pairings created a distinctly Oriental look. The patterns use themes of dragons and Oriental motifs, butterflies and insects, fish, flying humming birds, and fruit.

Often identification confusion arises when differentiating between Lustre Wares with similar patterns. For example, compare a Dragon Lustre piece with its mottled underglaze to a Lustre piece with Powder Blue ground and similar Dragon motif. Which is which? Are they both Dragon Lustre? Examining them, the ground on each differs, even in appearance. The Powder Blue ground has a textured look and the Dragon Lustre (as part of the Ordinary Lustre) will have a smoother, more streaky ground. The answer, according to the Wedgwood Museum at Barlaston, England, is yes; both can be called Dragon Lustre. Though the ground on each may differ, the design and overall look are the deciding factors. As seen in the next section, this is further complicated by the use of the name Fairyland as a blanket phrase for them all.

Bud vase, c. 1915. Dragon Lustre, blue with gold dragon designs and mother-of-pearl interior, pattern number Z4829, 5". *Author's Collection.* $210-240.

Commercial Lustre: Fairyland Lustre

Fairyland Lustre, introduced in 1915, is similar in composition to Ordinary Lustre, but with distinct design differences. The design themes involve more fantasy-like landscapes populated by imps and fairies, most often colored black or, in lesser quantities, white. The scenes and patterns follow a mythical premise of fictional places and creatures with Oriental influenced inspiration.

Here again we encounter the difficulties of identification. Though it may seem straightforward that these mythical themes would differentiate the Fairyland Lustre, we find that this is not strictly the case. The Wedgwood Museum states that the name Fairyland Lustre has become a blanket term representing a wide range of wares, including Ordinary Lustre.

Wedgwood's introduction of Ordinary Lustres (Fairyland Lustre) during World War I propelled Wedgwood ahead of its competitors. Lustre Ware became one of the most significant ceramic developments in the twentieth century and one that can be truly attributed to Wedgwood. Their production period however was brief. The American Stock Market crash of 1929 led to less expensive decorative wares being purchased. This reduced demand for Lustre pieces and led to dramatic cutbacks on the production at Wedgwood. Years later when the economy recovered, the industry had long since moved on to other stylistic directions.

Miscellaneous Lustre Designs

Daisy Makeig-Jones also worked with Celtic and Persian designs, which made some use of Lustre accents. These patterns were applied to tablewares and were not heavily produced.

Celtic art is generally comprised of intricate knot patterns and geometric figures of circles and spirals. These designs trace back to fifth and sixth century monasteries where religious icons, such as crosses and other forms of wood and metal art, were decorated with interwoven lines in intricate ways. The style was where Daisy Makeig-Jones looked for artistic inspiration.

Artist/Designer: S. M. Daisy Makeig-Jones

The most recognized name in the development and success of Wedgwood's twentieth century Lustre Ware is Susannah Margaretta "Daisy" Makeig-Jones. Daisy was an artist and designer who worked for Wedgwood from 1909-1931. She started as a painter in 1909 and worked up to Designer by 1911, where she brought together lustre grounds with gold gilt in fantasy designs. The success of Makeig-Jones's Fairyland Lustre propelled Wedgwood to a leadership status in the field of ornamental Bone China. Today her wares command high prices among antique collectors.

Makeig-Jones also designed a limited number of other works that derived their patterns for Persian and Hindu styled art. Similar to the Islamic-influenced wares created by Alfred and Louise Powell, Makeig-Jones embellished the designs with lustre to create a subtle Old World feel. Some of these original art works used as sources were metal chalices and footed bowls which Wedgwood recreated using mother-of-pearl coloring and silver highlighting.

Three Moonlight Lustre pieces, c. 1815. Large goblet, 5", $300-500. Moonlight Lustre plate, 8", $300-500. Small Moonlight Lustre goblet, 3.25", $250-400. *Courtesy of the Chellis and Adams Collection.*

Pink Lustre bowl, detailed view. *Courtesy of the Chellis and Adams Collection.*

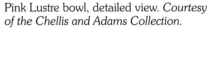

Pink Lustre bowl, c. 1810. Features reversible image (rotating the bowl 180 degrees reveals a different image), 6.25". *Courtesy of the Chellis and Adams Collection.* $250-350.

Nautilus shell wall pocket, c. 1810-1815. Moonlight Lustre, 9.5" x 6.25".
Courtesy of the Chellis and Adams Collection. $700-1,000.

Creamer, c. 1920s. Pink Lustre in the style of
Louise Powell. *Courtesy of the Chellis and
Adams Collection.* $100-150.

Pink Lustre cup, c. 1810.
*Courtesy of the Chellis and
Adams Collection.* $100-150.

Candlestick, c. 1815. Moonlight Lustre, "Wedgwood" impressed mark. *Courtesy of the Chellis and Adams Collection.* $100-175.

Pastille burner with cover, c. 1810. Ovoid-shaped body and tripod stand, copper (gold) Lustre finish. *Courtesy of the Chellis and Adams Collection.* $1,500-1,600.

Shell plate, c. 1810. Moonlight Lustre with mottled effect. *Courtesy of the Frazier Collection.* $150-200.

233

Pair of potpourri vases with pierced covers, c. 1810. Variegated Moonlight Lustre. *Courtesy of the Slavid Collection.* $1,200.

Potpourri jar cover missing, c. 1805. Moonlight Lustre, arabesque folic border marked: "Josiah Wedgwood 2nd February 1805," 4.25". *Courtesy of the Slavid Collection.* $1,000.

Creamer, c. 1950s. Ferrara pattern on a Creamware body with silver resist, augmented with Lustre decoration, pattern AL8870, 3". *Courtesy of the Keefe Collection.* $60-80.

Pitcher, c. 1950s. Creamware body with silver resist, grapevine designs, augmented with Lustre decoration, pattern CMH5869. *Courtesy of the Keefe Collection.* $80-100.

Hunt jug, c. 1950s. Creamware body with silver resist, augmented with Lustre decoration, pattern CMH5224. *Author's Collection.* $75-90.

Cup and saucer, c. 1960s. Pear shape design, Celadon colored,
augmented with silver resist. *Author's Collection*. $60-80.

Plant pot, c. 1940. Silver resist. *Courtesy
of the Frazier Collection*. $40-60.

Rhodian Ware box, c. 1926, with copper luster Islamic decoration, 6 5/8", $400-600, Rhodian Ware vase, c. 1930, with copper luster Islamic decoration, 6". *Courtesy of the Slavid Collection.* $300-400.

Footed chalice bowl, c. 1920. Hummingbird Lustre with mottled dark blue exterior and orange interior. *Courtesy of the Chellis and Adams Collection.* $1,700-2,100.

Bowl, c. 1920. Butterfly Lustre, shape 2454, with mottled orange and green Lustre, gilded butterfly images, and mother-of-pearl on the interior, 8 5/8". *Courtesy of the Horn and Hoffman Collection.* $600-700.

Bowl, interior view. *Courtesy of the Horn and Hoffman Collection.*

Jardinière, c. 1930-1935. Copper plated. *Courtesy of the Horn and Hoffman Collection.* $100-200.

Four Lustre bowls (one octagonal shaped, one full sized, and three minis). (Far left) Blue with orange interior, c. 1914-1928, $150-200. (Second from left) White Lustre with Mother-of-pearl interior, c. 1914-1928, $150-200. (Third from left) Green Lustre with light green interior, c. 1914-1928, $150-200. (Right, full-sized) Large, octagon shaped Dragon Lustre bowl, c. 1914-1928, blue with mother-of-pearl interior and Dragon Motifs, $1,000-1,300. *Courtesy of the Horn and Hoffman Collection.*

Three Lustre pieces: Butterfly Lustre Melba cup, c. 1920s, $400-450. Two mini round Lustre cups: (Left) green with mother-of-pearl interior, c. 1914-1928, $100-125. (Right) blue with orange interior, c. 1914-1928, $100-125. *Courtesy of the Horn and Hoffman Collection.*

Bowl. c 1815. Ruby red Butterfly Lustre with mother-of-pearl interior and butterfly decorations in gold. Marks: WEDGWOOD and the Portland Vase stamp. *Author's Collection.* $170-200.

Brooch, c. 1920. Fairyland Lustre with mother-of-pearl ground and flying fairy motif, metal backing and pin, 2". *Courtesy of the Slavid Collection.* $1,000.

Vase, c. 1917. Fairyland Lustre, shape 2442, with scene entitled *Castle on the Road*. This particular vase has a powder blue ground with copper-Lustre highlighting and black, gold, blue, purple, and green colors. *Courtesy of the Donald Eric Johnson Collection.* $2,500-3,500.

Salt cup, c. 1920. Fairyland Lustre depicting two fawns grazing, 3". *Courtesy of the Slavid Collection.* $850.

Bowl, c. 1915-1930. Fairyland Lustre, gold trim. *Courtesy of the Slavid Collection*. $1,000.

Fairyland Lustre Bowl, interior view. *Courtesy of the Slavid Collection*.

Two Fairyland Lustre cups, c. 1920. Fairy motifs on night sky background with mother-of-pearl interiors and gold trim: (Left) York Cup, "Z4968 leapfrog elves," 4.75", $900-1,200. (Right) Boston Cup, 4", $800-1,200. *Courtesy of the Slavid Collection*.

Chapter 10
Other Ceramic Wares

Wedgwood has produced numerous ceramic forms in many styles over the course of their history. Invariably branches, sub-groups, and experimental techniques fall outside the more mainstream product lines. The following categories are those that were not in mainstream production, nor were they purposely made for any length of time. They all have one thing in common, they each utilized similar Parian-type ceramic bodies.

Carrara (Parian) Ware

The mid-nineteenth century saw a period of artistic growth in Europe. Items produced during this period

Carrara bust, c. 1858. Depicting Robert Stevenson by E. W. Wyon. *Courtesy of the Frazier Collection*. $850-1,000.

included elaborate and detailed statues, groups, and busts, made from marble and other semi-precious stones, which were in vogue amongst the European aristocracy. England's middle class could not afford such works, which opened an opportunity for European potters to produce affordable substitutes.

The pottery industry responded with Parian: a clay simulation of marble that was molded quickly into shapes rather than laboriously chiseled as were their marble counterparts. Parian was a creamy white, smooth, and porcelain-like ceramic. Its surface had a natural semi-translucent sheen that was perfect for figures and busts without any added coloring or glazing. Parian busts, statues, and groups could now be mass-produced at a reasonable cost and they even had an appeal to the aristocracy.

Wedgwood introduced its own version of Parian in 1849, called Carrara Statuary Porcelain or simply Carrara. The name Carrara was taken from its close resemblance to the marble from the quarries around Carrara in Northern Italy. Since the Parian name was the widely accepted industry term and Carrara was a specifically Wedgwood name, it was not uncommon that the Parian and Carrara names were used interchangeably when describing these types of Wedgwood wares. Carrara production continued at Wedgwood until the early 1890s.

Artist: Edward William Wyon
Edward William Wyon was a sculptor working for Wedgwood in the mid-1800s. He focused primarily on sculpting Carrara figures and busts, though he also produced a number of busts in Black Basalt. Wyon's busts often have his name etched in the back of each bust, particularly on the larger library sized versions.

Victoria Ware

In 1861, Wedgwood experimented with a glazed form of Carrara that looked similar to Majolica. The difference between Carrara and Majolica was in the traditional styles and relief decoration more characteristic of that of Basalt and Jasper creations. Victoria Ware began as vase shapes that had colored grounds and gilded highlights, as well as a heavily ornamented relief. This glazing on Carrara was used mainly between 1866-1880 to compete with Minton's Majolica. Though the manufacturing costs of Carrara and Majolica were not substantially different on their own, when the added cost of then glazing was taken into account, it made the Carrara more expensive. Majolica also used a less expensive earthenware body under the glaze. Due to Carrara's expense, Wedgwood dropped the glazed Carrara in favor of the less expensive Majolica.

Victoria Ware shapes consisted mainly of ornamental pieces, reminiscent of eighteenth and early nineteenth century shapes used for Wedgwood's Jasper and Basalt ceramic bodies. Except for the colorful enameled finish, Victoria Ware designs resembled those of Jasper in style. In fact, Wedgwood often reused old Jasper and Basalt molds for Victoria Ware shapes. Some of these Victoria Ware pieces have been known to include a printed Portland Vase mark similar to those on Bone China of the same period.

Vase, 1899. Green Victoria Ware, glazed and gilded. (OMB mark). *Courtesy of the Frazier Collection.* $400-500.

Pâte-sur-Pâte

Pâte-sur-Pâte was a slip layering technique developed in France in 1841. It started with a colored ground, usually a flat object like a plaque. Layers of ultra-thin slip were then painted on in layers, building up a semi-transparent layered relief. The relief details are carved, or undercut, in the built up relief prior to the piece being fired. The result was a delicate, exceptionally detailed, and translucent design.

Though this book does not contain any examples of Pâte-sur-Pate, it is necessary to cover it due to the frequent confusion in distinguishing Pâte-sur-Pâte and similar looking Victoria Wares. Victoria Ware is somewhat difficult to find in today's antiques market; Pâte-sur-Pâte examples are even more scarce. Relatively speaking, Pâte-sur-Pâte is much more expensive than Victoria Ware due to its limited supply and laborious techniques involved in its creation.

One of the foremost artists who worked with Pâte-sur-Pâte was French artist Marc Louis Emanuel Solon. Minton hired Solon in 1870 in order to bring his knowledge to English potteries. In 1877, Wedgwood hired artist Frederick A. Rhead, who studied under Solon, to produce a Wedgwood version of Pâte-sur-Pâte. Rhead produced his own version of Pâte-sur-Pâte, utilizing Wedgwood's white Carrara body as the base. Wedgwood introduced Rhead's Pâte-sur-Pâte in 1878, primarily in the form of plaques with Greek female figures as their main subject. Other companies have produced various shapes of Pâte-sur-Pâte, such as vases, but due of the difficulty of producing objects with layered relief, Wedgwood stayed with flatter objects like plaques and tablets.

The composition of Pâte-sur-Pâte and Victoria Ware is quite similar, both utilizing a Carrara body and colored enamels. The key difference is in the design. As mentioned, the relief in Victoria Ware was produced from molds much in the same way as Jasper so the relief appears uniform from piece to piece. This mold technique does not have the level of detail and is not as impressive as the handmade Pâte-sur-Pâte. Due to the labor-intensive nature of the process, only a limited production of Pâte-sur-Pâte was made and was discontinued in 1880. Today Pâte-sur-Pâte wares are difficult to locate and command high prices due to their scarceness and incredibly lengthy process to produce. In 2002, Wedgwood again produced a very limited amount of Pâte-sur-Pâte, primarily for the Japanese market.

Carrara bust, c. 1859. Depicting James Watt, sculpted by E. W. Wyon, 15". *Courtesy of the Horn and Hoffman Collection.* $600-700.

Carrara bust, c. 1860s. Depicting Sir Walter Scott, notice intricate plaid detail in clothing, sculpted by E. W. Wyon. *Courtesy of the Horn and Hoffman Collection.* $600-700.

Carrara bust, c. 1860. Depicting Byron, sculpted by E. W. Wyon. *Courtesy of the Horn and Hoffman Collection.* $750-950.

Carrara bust, c. 1864. Depicting Shakespeare, designed by Felix Martin Miller, 16". Written on back: "The Shakespeare Memorial Bust, Published under the special sanction of the National Shakespeare and Stratford-On-Avon tercentenary committee" commissioned by Howell Jane & Co. London April 23 1864 for Shakespeare Tercentenary 4/23/1864." *Courtesy of the Horn and Hoffman Collection.* $600-800.

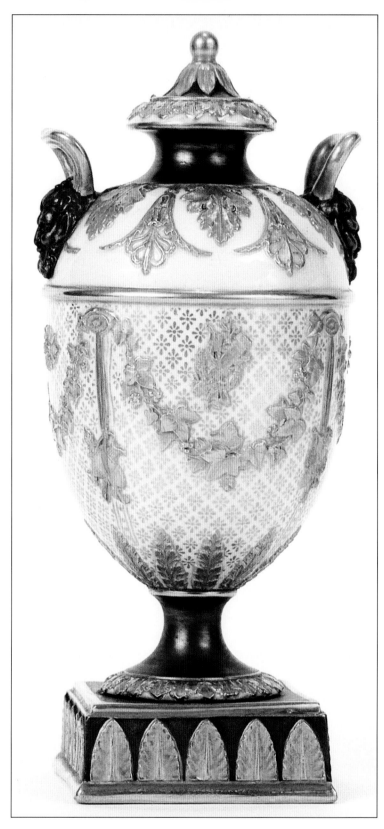

Barber bottle, c. 1880. Victoria Ware with cobalt blue
background, white swags, and maroon medallions.
Courtesy of the Horn and Hoffman Collection. $700-800.

Covered vase, c. 1880. Victoria Ware, French styled
design with gilt swags and trophies. *Courtesy of the
Horn and Hoffman Collection.* $600-800.

Two-handled vase with cover, c. 1880.
Victoria Ware with polychrome green,
coral, black, and turquoise coloring,
7.25". *Courtesy of the Horn and Hoffman
Collection.* $600-800.

Wedgwood Chronology

c. 1750   Josiah Wedgwood begins experimentation with Earthenware.

Salt Glazed Stoneware in production.

1752   Transfer printing invented by John Sadler.

1754   Wedgwood enters into partnership with Thomas Whieldon.

Transfer printing patented.

1759   Wedgwood partnership with Thomas Whieldon ends.

Variegated Ware (solid agate and surface glazed) introduced.

c. 1760   Green Glazed Ware introduced.

1760   Creamware introduced.

1761   Transfer printing on Queen's Ware introduced.

Wedgwood partners with Sadler & Green on transfer printing.

1763   Production of Salt-Glazed Ware is discontinued.

1766   Wedgwood's Creamware renamed Queen's Ware.

1767   Josiah Wedgwood begins experimentation with Black clays

1768   Wedgwood enters into partnership with Thomas Bentley.

Wedgwood introduces Black Porcelain (later renamed Basalt).

1769   Wedgwood patents and introduces Encaustic Painted decoration on Basalt.

Sculptor William Hackwood begins work at Wedgwood.

1770   Wedgwood introduces Cane Ware.

Wedgwood introduces Bamboo-styled Cane Ware.

Wedgwood introduces Encaustic Painted decoration on Cane Ware.

Wedgwood introduces Enameled Decoration Cane Ware.

1771   Josiah Wedgwood begins experimentation with Jasper.

1775   The Frog Service completed for Catherine the Great.

Wedgwood introduces solid Jasper.

1776   Production of Green Glazed Ware is discontinued.

Wedgwood introduces Jasper Dip.

Wedgwood introduces Rosso Antico.

1779   Green Glazed Ware production reintroduced in small quantities.

Wedgwood introduces Pearl Ware.

1780   Artist George Stubbs produces famous Basalt plaques of the *Frightened Horse* and the *Fall of Phaeton.*

Thomas Bentley passes away and with him the Wedgwood-Bentley partnership.

1783   Wedgwood reintroduces Cane Ware with a more consistent formula.

1785   Wedgwood introduces Dice Ware.

1787   Wedgwood produces the Slave Medallion.

1790   Wedgwood produces their first Portland Vase.

1795   Josiah Wedgwood passes away.

Wedgwood introduces Pastry Ware (a.k.a. Piecrust Ware) and Game Pie Dishes.

1799   Wedgwood partnership with Sadler & Green on transfer printing ends.

1800   Production of Variegated Ware (marbled) is discontinued.

Production of Encaustic Painted decoration on Cane Ware is discontinued.

Production of Enameled Decoration on Cane Ware is discontinued.

1805   Wedgwood introduces modified Queen's Ware.

Wedgwood introduces White Ware as well as a thicker version, Chamber Ware.

Production of Pastry Ware is discontinued.

Wedgwood introduces Pink Lustre, Purple Lustre, and Moonlight Lustre.

1806   Wedgwood introduces Underglaze on Pearl Ware.

1810   Wedgwood introduces Enameled Decoration on Basalt.

1811   Wedgwood introduces Blue Underglaze.

1812   Wedgwood introduces Bone China, decorated in the Regency Style.

1815   Wedgwood introduces limited production of Smear-glaze.

1817   Wedgwood introduces Bas-relief Ware.

Wedgwood produces first experimental piece of Stone China.

1820   Wedgwood introduces Drab Tableware (Drab Wear) as a stained Earthenware.

1822	Production of Bone China (first period) is discontinued.
1832	Sculptor William Hackwood ends work at Wedgwood.
1833	Production of Green Glazed Ware is discontinued.
1839	Wedgwood produces a brief line of Portland Vases featuring clothed figures.
1849	Wedgwood introduces Carrara (Parian) Ware.
c. 1850	Artist Edward William Wyon begins work with Wedgwood.
1858	Wedgwood introduces stained Creamware in Celadon and lavender colors.
	Artist Emile Lessore begins work with Wedgwood.
1859	Wedgwood introduces the Cambridge Ale Jug shape in Rosso Antico.
c. 1860	Production of Drab Tableware (Drab Ware) is discontinued.
1860	Wedgwood introduces Majolica (using lead-based glazes).
1861	Production of Stone China is discontinued.
	Wedgwood produces first experimental pieces of Victoria Ware.
1862	Artist Harry Barnard begins work at Wedgwood.
1876	Artist Emile Lessore passes away.
	Artist Thomas Allen begins work with Wedgwood.
1877	Wedgwood and John Northwood (Stourbridge Glass) partner to produce 15 limited edition Portland Vases later known as Northwood Portland Vases.
	Artist Frederick A. Rhead begins work with Wedgwood.
	Wedgwood introduces Pâte-sur-Pâte.
1878	Production of Majolica (using lead-based glazes) is discontinued.
	Wedgwood introduces Majolica (using lower lead glazes).
	Wedgwood introduces Second Period Bone China.
1879	Jones McDuffee & Stratton, Co. and Wedgwood partner to produce calendar tiles.
1880s	Wedgwood introduces the Cambridge Ale Jug shape in Basalt.
1880	Production of Victoria Ware is discontinued.
	Production of Pâte-sur-Pâte is discontinued.
1881	Wedgwood introduces Marsden Ware.
1882	Celadon stain color briefly seen on Bone China.
	Calendar tiles produced depicting Bonner's Map of Boston, MA.
1885	Wedgwood introduces into brief production Auro Basalt.
	Wedgwood introduces into brief production Golconda Ware.
1887	Calendar tiles produced depicting the S.S. *Britannia* and S.S. *Etruria*.
1888	Production of Marsden Ware is discontinued.
c. 1890	Production of Chamber Ware is discontinued.
1891	Due to tariff restrictions, Wedgwood begins adding the word "England" to their marks.
1895	Wedgwood introduces Kenlock Ware.
1896	Calendar tiles produced in polychrome.
1898	Freelance Artist Clare Leighton begins work with Wedgwood.
	Wedgwood begins adding the words "Made in England" to their marks.
1899	Freelance Artist Clare Leighton ends work with Wedgwood.
1899	Wedgwood introduces Old Blue Historical Plates.
Early 1900s	Briefly revival in production of Drab Wares.
	Artists Alfred and Louise Powell begin work with Wedgwood.
1900	Variegated Ware (surface glazed) production is discontinued.
	Production of Kenlock Ware is discontinued.
	Production of Rosso Antico is discontinued.
1901	Production of Game Pie Dishes is discontinued.
1909	Artist/Designer S. M. Daisy Makeig-Jones begins work with Wedgwood.
1910	Production of Majolica (using lower lead glazes).
	Wedgwood introduces into brief production crimson colored Jasper.
1912	Wedgwood introduces Powder Blue Bone China.
1913	Wedgwood commissions Artist Ernest William Light to sculpt a series of animal figures.
1915	Wedgwood introduces Fairyland Lustre.
1917	Wedgwood produces the Liberty Ware Service.
	Wedgwood hires Artist Millicent J. Taplin.
1918	Production of Liberty Ware Service is discontinued.
c. 1920	Wedgwood designer S. M. Daisy Makeig-Jones introduces a new lustre called Commercial Ware Lustre.
1920	Wedgwood reintroduces Green Glazed Ware in pineapple and cauliflower designs.
	Wedgwood introduces into brief production olive colored Jasper.
	Wedgwood produces Rhodian Ware.
1925	Wedgwood introduces into brief production crimson colored Jasper.
1926	Freelance Sculptor John Skeaping creates animal sculpture in Basalt for Wedgwood.
1929	Production of calendar tiles is discontinued.

	Wedgwood introduces buff colored Jasper (Dip) with black relief.	1954	Wedgwood reintroduces Unique Wares in limited production.
1930	Production of Green Glazed Ware in pineapple and cauliflower designs are discontinued.	1957	Wedgwood introduces stained Creamware in cane color.
	Wedgwood introduces stained Creamware in honey buff color.		Wedgwood produces terracotta colored Jasper.
	Production of Rhodian Ware ended.	1958	Wedgwood introduces the Piranesi plates.
	Artists Alfred and Louise Powell end work with Wedgwood.	1959	Production of terracotta colored Jasper is discontinued.
1931	Artist/Designer S. M. Daisy Makeig-Jones end work with Wedgwood.	1963	Wedgwood Artist Millicent J. Taplin retires.
	Freelance Artist Erling (Eric) B. Olsen begins work with Wedgwood.	1963	Production of Unique Wares is discontinued.
1932	Production of crimson colored Jasper is discontinued.	1969	Wedgwood produces the Spanish Don decanters for the George G. Sandeman & Sons Company.
1933	Wedgwood introduces Matte Glazed Ware.	1970	Wedgwood produces another run of the Spanish Don decanters for the George G. Sandeman & Sons Company in honor of the Kentucky Derby.
	Artist Keith Murray begins full-time work at Wedgwood.		Wedgwood contracts with freelance Artist Eduardo L. Paolozzi to design a limited edition set of six Bone China plates called *Variations on a Geometric Theme*.
	Wedgwood introduces Veronese Glazed Ware.		
	Production of buff colored Jasper with black relief is discontinued.		
	Artist Harry Barnard ends work at Wedgwood.	1976	Wedgwood produced a limited trial of primrose yellow colored Japser.
1932	Wedgwood introduces Unique Wares.	1977	Wedgwood produces their third and final run of the Spanish Don decanters for the George G. Sandeman & Sons Company in conjunction with the celebration of Queen Elizabeth's Royal Silver Jubilee.
1934	Freelance Artist/Potter Victor Skellern begins work with Wedgwood.		
	Freelance Sculptor Alan Best creates athletic sculptures for Wedgwood.		
1935	Freelance Artist Erling (Eric) B. Olsen ends work with Wedgwood.	1980	Wedgwood produces limited edition Portland Vases to commemorate the 250th birthday of Josiah Wedgwood.
	Freelance Artist/Potter Eric Ravilious begins work with Wedgwood.	1983	Wedgwood has limited production of taupe colored Jasper as well and teal colored Jasper.
	Wedgwood reissues animal figures sculpted by Artist Ernest William Light.		
1936	Wedgwood introduces Alpine Pink Bone China.	1989	Wedgwood produces limited edition Portland Vases to commemorate the 200th anniversary of Josiah Wedgwood's perfecting the Portland Vase.
1939	Production of Unique Wares is discontinued.		
1940	Production of Pearl Ware is discontinued.	c. 1990	Wedgwood has a brief production of terracotta colored Jasper.
	Artist Keith Murray ends work at Wedgwood.	1995	In commemoration of Josiah Wedgwood's death, Wedgwood releases Frog Service reproductions.
1941	Production of Veronese Glazed Ware is discontinued.		
1942	Freelance Artist/Potter Eric Ravilious is killed in WWII.	1998	Wedgwood produces commemorative reproductions of the Frog Service as part of the Genius Collection.
1944	Freelance Artist Margaret Philbrick begins work with Wedgwood though her position with Jones McDuffee & Stratton, Co.	1999	Wedgwood revives production of Matt Glazed Ware for designs by fashion designer Paul Costelloe.
1944	Freelance Artist Margaret Philbrick ends work with Wedgwood.		
Mid-1900s	Hand painting and transfer printing on Queen's Ware is discontinued.	Late 1990s	Wedgwood introduces cane colored Jasper inspired by the 1700s Cane Ware.
1953	Wedgwood introduces stained Creamware in Windsor grey color.	2002	Wedgwood revives production of Pâte-sur-Pâte for the Japanese market.
	Wedgwood introduces Royal blue colored Jasper to commemorate the coronation of Queen Elizabeth II, including Portland Vase designs.		

Bibliography

Adams, Elizabeth Bryding. *The Dwight and Lucille Beeson Wedgwood Collection at The Birmingham Museum of Art*. Birmingham, Alabama: Birmingham Museum of Art, 1992.

Allen, H. "Wedgwood Hieroglyphics." *The American Wedgwoodian Vol. 1 No.1, August 1962*. New York, NY: Wedgwood International Seminar, 1962.

Allen, Harold. "Egyptian Influences in Wedgwood Designs." *The Seventh Wedgwood International Seminar Proceedings*. New York, New York: Wedgwood International Seminar, 1962.

Barnard, Harry. *Chats on Wedgwood Ware*. New York, New York: Frederick A. Stokes Co., 1924.

Batkin, Maureen. *Wedgwood Ceramics 1846-1959 A New Appraisal*. London, England: Richard Dennis, 1982.

Burton, Anthony. *Josiah Wedgwood*. New York: Stien and Day/Publishers Scarborough House, 1976.

Burton, William. *Josiah Wedgwood and His Pottery*. New York, New York: Funk and Wagnalls Co., 1922.

Buten, David. *18th-Century Wedgwood A Guide for Collectors & Connoisseurs*. New York, New York: Methuen, Inc., 1980.

Buten, David. "Wedgwood's Encaustic-Painted Vases." *The Twenty-First Wedgwood International Seminar*. New York, New York: Wedgwood International Seminar, 1976.

Buten, David & Patricia Pelehach. *Emile Lessore 1805-1876: His Life and Work*. Merion, Pennsylvania: The Buten Museum of Wedgwood, 1979.

Buten, David & Patricia Pelehach. *Wedgwood and America – Wedgwood Bas-relief Ware – Monographs in Wedgwood Studies, Nos. 1 & 2*. Merion, Pennsylvania: The Buten Museum of Wedgwood, 1977.

Buten, Harry M. *Wedgwood ABC But Not Middle E*. Merion, Pennsylvania: The Buten Museum of Wedgwood, 1964.

Buten, Harry M. *Wedgwood and Artists*. Merion, Pennsylvania: The Buten Museum of Wedgwood, 1960.

Buten, Harry M. *Wedgwood Counterpoint*. Merion, Pennsylvania: The Buten Museum of Wedgwood, 1962.

Buten, Harry M. *Wedgwood Rarities*. Merion, Pennsylvania: The Buten Museum of Wedgwood, 1969.

Buten, Harry M. "Wedgwood Bone China Marks." *The American Wedgwoodian Vol. 2 No. 6, April 1967*.

New York, New York: Wedgwood International Seminar, 1967.

Childs, Emily R. "The Don Decanter: A Wedgwood Premium." *The BMW Bulletin. Vol. 6, No. 3. October 1982*. Merion, Pennsylvania: The Buten Museum of Wedgwood, 1982.

Connelly, John. *A Century of Uninterrupted Progress*. n.p., n.d.

Cox, Warren E. *The Book of Pottery and Porcelain Volume 1*. New York, New York: Crown Publishers, 1944.

Dawson, Aileen. *Masterpieces of Wedgwood in the British Museum*. London, England: British Museum Publications, 1984.

Dennis, Richard. *Ravilious and Wedgwood – The Complete Wedgwood Designs of Eric Ravilious*. Somerset, England: Richard Dennis (reprint), 1995.

Edwards, Diana. *Black Basalt – Wedgwood and Contemporary Manufacturers*. Suffolk, England: Antique Collectors' Club, 1994.

Edwards, Diana & Rodney Hampson. *English Dry-Bodied Stoneware – Wedgwood and Contemporary Manufacturers 1774-1830*. Suffolk, England: Antique Collectors' Club, 1998.

Finer, Ann & George Savage (Editors). *The Selected Letters of Josiah Wedgwood*. New York, New York: The Born & Hawes Publishing Co., 1965.

Fontaines, Una des. *Wedgwood Fairyland Lustre The Work of Daisy Makeig-Jones*. New York, New York: Born-Hawes Publishing Limited, 1975.

Frazier, Ronald F. "Interview with a Wedgwood Artist: Margaret Philbrick." *Ars Ceramica 1995, Number 12*. Glen Head, New York: The Wedgwood Society of New York, 1995.

Gibson, Michael. *Lustreware*. England: Shire Publications Ltd., 1993.

Gorely, Jean. *Wedgwood*. New York: Gramercy Publishing Co., 1950.

Graham II, John Meredith and Cecil Hensleigh Wedgwood. *Wedgwood A Living Tradition*. New York, New York: John B. Watkins Company, 1948.

Kelly, Alison. *Wedgwood Ware*. London, England: Ward Lock Ltd., 1970.

King, Jean Callan. "English Majolica." *The Twenty-Seventh Wedgwood International Seminar Proceedings*.

New York, New York: Wedgwood International Seminar, 1982.

Macht, Carol. *Classical Wedgwood Designs*. New York: M. Barrows and Company, 1957.

Mankowitz, Wolf. *The Portland Vase & The Wedgwood Copies*. London, England: Andre Deutsch Limited, 1952.

Mankowitz, Wolf. *Wedgwood*. London, England: The Hamlyn Publishing Group Limited (reprint), 1966.

Meteyard, Eliza. *The Wedgwood Handbook*. Pekskill, New York: Timothy Trace (reprint), 1963.

Reilly, Robin. *The Collector's Wedgwood*. Huntington, New York: Portfolio Press, 1980.

Reilly, Robin. *The New Illustrated Dictionary*. Woodbridge, Suffolk, England: Antique Collectors' Club, 1995.

Reilly, Robin. *Wedgwood Volume 1 & Volume 2*. New York, New York: Stockton Press, 1989.

Roberts, Gaye Blake. "Basalt and Jasper." *Wedgwood: Art, Design, & Production*. Toronto, Canada: Wedgwood International Seminar, 2002.

Smith, L. Richard. *Josiah Wedgwood's Slave Medallion*. Australia: The Wedgwood Society of New South Wales Inc., 1999.

Simcox, Jacqueline & W. D. John Simcox. *Early Wedgwood Lustre Wares*. England: The Ceramic Book Company, 1963.

Tattersall, Bruce. *Stubbs & Wedgwood – Unique alliance between Artist and Potter*. London, England: The Tate Gallery Publications Department, 1974.

Wedgwood, Hensleigh C. "The Contributions of Norman Wilson to the Modernization of Wedgwood in the Twentieth Century." *The Twenty-Sixth Wedgwood International Seminar Proceedings*. New York, New York: Wedgwood International Seminar, 1981.

Williams, Peter. *Wedgwood - A Collector's Guide*. Radnor, Pennsylvania: Quintet Publishing Ltd., 1992.

Wills, Geoffrey. *Wedgwood*. Secaucus, New Jersey: Chartwell Books, Inc., 1989.

Appendix

Three Letter Marks

A number of the piece descriptions in this book have a three letter mark. Wedgwood began using these marks in 1860. These marks can be very useful when you already know the general time period when the piece was produced, but you are looking to exactly pinpoint the month and year of production.

To help identify the date: use the first letter of the mark which indicates the month of production and the last letter which represents the year produced. (The letter in the middle represents the potter of the piece). An example would be an Emile Lessore hand-painted Queen's Ware piece produced during his time at Wedgwood, which was 1858-1875. The piece has a three letter mark of "FOX." The "F" indicates the month of February and the "X" indicates 1869, so the piece was produced in February of 1869.

First letter mark indicating Month

Month	
January	J
February	F
March	M (M was used from 1860-1863)
	R (R was used from 1864-1907)
April	A
May	Y (Y was used from 1860-1863)
	M (M was used from 1864-1907)
June	T
July	V (V was used from 1860-1863)
	L (L was used from 1864-1907)
August	W
September	S
October	O
November	N
December	D

Third letter mark indicating Year

Year		Year		Year	
1860	O	1884	M	1907	J
1861	P	1885	N	1908	K
1862	Q	1886	O	1909	L
1863	R	1887	P	1910	M
1864	S	1888	Q	1911	N
1865	T	1889	R	1912	O
1866	U	1890	S	1913	P
1867	V	1891	T	1914	Q
1868	W	1892	U	1915	R
1869	X	1893	V	1916	S
1870	Y	1894	W	1917	T
1871	Z	1895	X	1918	U
1872	A	1896	Y	1919	V
1873	B	1897	Z	1920	W
1874	C	1898	A	1921	X
1875	D	1899	B	1922	Y
1876	E	1900	C	1923	Z
1877	F	1901	D	1924	A
1878	G	1902	E	1925	B
1879	H	1903	F	1926	C
1880	I	1904	G	1927	D
1881	J	1905	H	1928	E
1882	K	1906	I	1929	F
1883	L				

Notes to the dating process:

In 1891 the word "England" was added to the marks in conjunction with the McKinley Tariff Act. In 1898 they started putting Made in England on the pieces.

In 1907, the month letter was replaced with a constant number "3" and then in 1924 the month number was again replaced with a constant number "4."

After 1929, Wedgwood no longer used three letter marks and began new dating systems.

Index

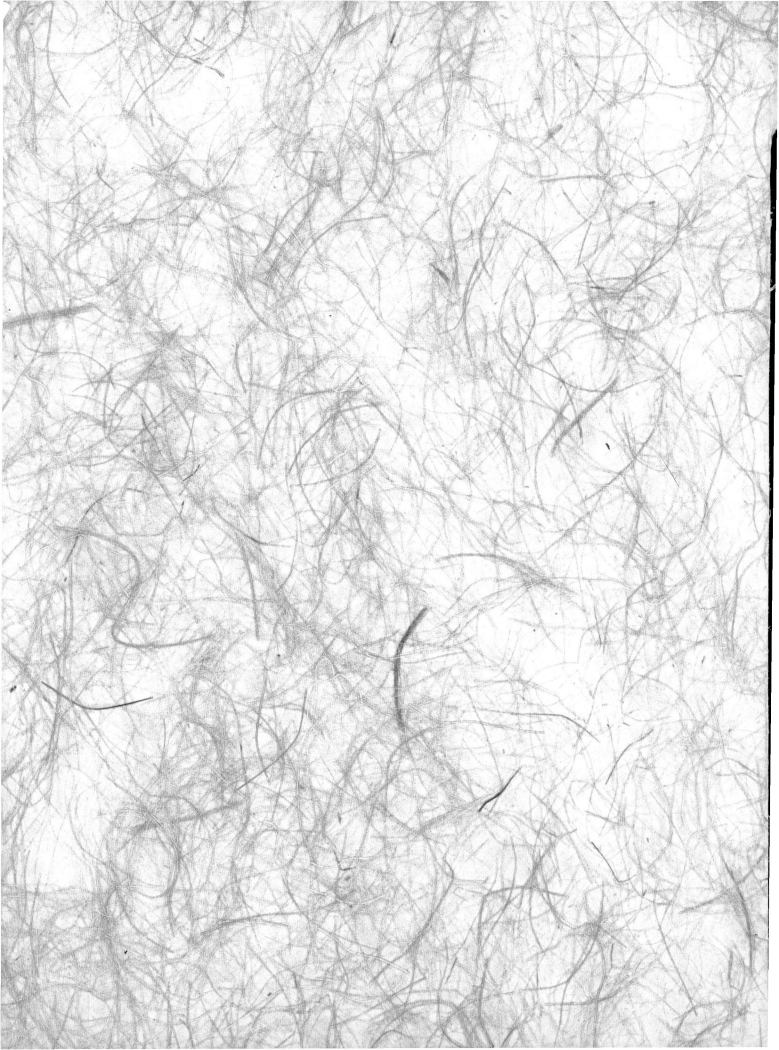